ALAN G. HODGKISS

# Discovering
# Antique Maps

SHIRE PUBLICATIONS LTD

## ACKNOWLEDGEMENTS

I am greatly indebted to the late Professor J. B. Harley for his kindness in lending his expert knowledge to the reading of my original manuscript. Ian Qualtrough has applied his photographic skills generously to the difficult task of photographing early maps. I am especially grateful to him. Katy Hooper of the Special Collections section of the Liverpool University Library has been unfailingly helpful in making available for photography early maps from the University's splendid collection. Professor R. Lawton permitted me to reproduce maps from the collection of the Department of Geography, University of Liverpool. Other illustrations are reproduced from maps in my own collection.

Cover: *Detail from 'Dorcestriae', Christopher Saxton's map of Dorset in 'An Atlas of England and Wales', London, 1579.*

British Library Cataloguing in Publication Data: Hodgkiss, Alan G. Discovering Antique Maps. – 5Rev. ed.– (Discovering Series; No. 98) I. Title II. Series 912.42

*Published in 1996 by Shire Publications Ltd, Cromwell House, Church Street, Princes Risborough, Buckinghamshire HP27 9AA, UK.*
*Copyright © 1996 by Alan Hodgkiss. First published 1971. Further editions in 1975, 1977 and 1981. Fourth edition reprinted 1983, 1986, 1988 and 1992. Fifth edition, completely revised and expanded, published 1996. Number 98 in the Discovering series. ISBN 0 7478 0307 2.*
*Alan Hodgkiss is hereby identified as the author of this work in accordance with Section 77 of the Copyright, Designs and Patents Act 1988.*

Printed in Great Britain by CIT Printing Services, Press Buildings, Merlins Bridge, Haverfordwest, Dyfed SA61 1XF.

# Contents

# Introduction

'What greater pleasure can there now bee, than to view those elaborate maps of Ortelius, Mercator, etc... Me thinks it would well please any man to look upon a Geographical map...to behold as it were all the Remote Provinces, Townes, Cities of the World'. *Anatomy of Melancholy*, Robert Burton, 1621.

Burton admirably sums up the author's own affection for maps and for early maps in particular. Evidence that not everyone takes the same view, however, is provided in the following quotation from Robert Louis Stevenson's *Treasure Island*: 'I am told that there are people who do not care for maps and find it hard to believe. The names, the shapes...the courses of the roads and rivers...are an inexhaustible fund of interest for any man with eyes to see or two-penceworth of imagination to understand with.' Many people are simply charmed by the decorative attributes of an early map by Speed or Blaeu and like to have examples of such maps displayed on the wall of their living room or study. While early maps are certainly highly decorative – indeed, there was a time not so long ago when people turned them into lampshades – they have so much more to offer than mere decoration. Basically they were designed to demonstrate graphically the geographical knowledge of their day but additionally they often include an illustration of the customs and costume of the area under consideration; their ornamentation reflects contemporary artistic style and taste; their colouring is often brilliant and the profession of map colourist was a highly respected one.

The development of mapmaking techniques makes a very interesting study and the lives of the men who made the maps is often highly illuminating: Mercator, for instance, was not only a respected geographer but also an instrument maker, engraver and scribe who developed his own scripts specifically for mapmaking. He was also, at one time, accused of being a heretic; he invented a famous map projection which bears his name and is still in constant use today; and he was the man who used the word 'Atlas' for the first time to denote a bound collection of maps. John Ogilby, maker of fine maps and roadbooks, was another remarkable character whose extraordinarily varied career encompassed the roles of choreographer and dancing master, theatre manager and translator of the classics, and who contributed much to fine bookmaking in England, produced travel books and introduced the still popular 'strip map' method of depicting roads in 1675.

People may or may not be excited by maps. Nevertheless, maps and atlases have been enthusiastically collected since Tudor times when many early maps, often salvaged from the breakup of medieval libraries at the time of the dissolution of the monasteries, were incorporated into private collections such as those of Archbishop Matthew Parker and Sir Robert Cotton. William Cecil, first Lord Burghley, gathered together a notable collection of maps which provided him with valuable reference material to assist him in carrying out his duties in Public Administration in his capacity as Secretary of State and Lord High Treasurer. Samuel Pepys was another assiduous collector and noted sadly in his diary for 19th September 1666: 'I am mightily troubled, and even in my sleep, at my missing Speed's *Chronicle* and a book of charts, which I suppose I have put up with too much care that I forget where they are' – a situation with which many of us are all too familiar!

In the late eighteenth and early nineteenth centuries a number of scholar/collectors emerged. Alfred Nordenskiöld, born in Helsinki of Swedish parents, was a splendid example whose judicious collecting provided research material, not only for his own published work, *Facsimile-Atlas to the Early History of Cartography* (1889) for example, but for generations of future scholars. The systematic study of early cartography also prospered in Europe as a consequence of the emerging national map collections and institutional collections in universities, government departments, geographical societies and important libraries. Such institutions provided homes for valuable map collections such as that of the antiquary Richard Gough, which is cared for in the Bodleian Library, Oxford.

The modern boom in early map collecting, as far as it relates to the amateur, man-in-the-street collector, probably dates to the 1920s. Today map collecting has become so popular that it enjoys a society of its own, the International Map Collectors' Society (IMCOS), and a first-class journal, *The Map Collector*, which features articles on the history of cartography together with reviews, news items, auction prices and so on. In addition numerous regional and local societies are flourishing, particularly in the United States.

Some collectors look upon early maps as a form of investment and prices have rocketed since the 1950s when a seventeenth-century county map by Blaeu could be purchased for around thirty shillings. Others base their collection on a particular theme: maps of a specific area in which they are interested, often their home county; the work of a specific mapmaker or school of mapmaking; maps from a particular period; or a collection devoted to a study of individual features such as the cartouche or ornamental title panel. A collection systematically assembled to a theme has greater value in every sense than one put together haphazardly.

Nowadays there are many specialist dealers in early maps, some of whom are listed at the end of this book. A more complete list will be found in the *International Directory of Map Dealers* issued by Map Collector Publications (1982) Ltd. Rare atlases appear at specialised auction sales by the leading auction houses. General antique dealers sometimes have early maps in stock; so too have antiquarian booksellers, and there are still occasional bargains to be sought out by the keen collector. Whatever the motive for collecting, the rewards will be generous in one way or another.

Cartography, the art and science of mapmaking (for it falls into both categories), has a long, multi-faceted history, the whole field of which would need several very large volumes to do it any sort of justice. The present work can attempt only to provide readers with an introduction to the subject and, it is hoped, encourage them to further investigations. In the opening section the terminology of early maps and their constituent features will be considered. This will be followed by a resumé of landmarks in cartographic development leading up to the end of the sixteenth century. The remainder of the book will concentrate on mapmaking in Europe, British regional mapmaking from Saxton's time onwards, and will take a look at urban plans, route maps and nautical charts. The emphasis will be on the printed map though some early manuscript maps will be mentioned briefly.

## *What is meant by an 'original' map?*

Collectors are sometimes concerned as to how they can distinguish an 'original' map from a high-quality modern facsimile reproduction, so it is appropriate that something should be said about the term 'original' as applied to early maps. Prior to the invention of printing from wood blocks and, later, from engraved copper plates, maps were drawn on vellum, sheepskin or other suitable material and could be reproduced only by laborious hand copying. Further classes of map, for example the estate map, may have been produced in manuscript only, with no printing process involved. So far, therefore, the word 'original' may be applied in just the same way as it would be to a painting, i.e. in the sense of an individual, unique piece of artwork. The advent of the printing process, however, allowed the production of multiple copies and when printed maps are under discussion the word 'original' refers to a *print* or *impression* taken from a wood block or a copper or steel plate. This is what is normally meant by an 'original' map – a print and not a single, unique piece of artwork.

The earliest printed maps were impressions taken from engravings on wood blocks – a *relief* process in which detail and lettering were left standing to form a printing surface and those areas without detail were cut away. The ensuing development, that of engraving maps on sheets of copper, brought greater flexibility and precision into mapmaking, so that lettering became more flowing and detail could be finer and neater. Copper engraving is an *intaglio* process, the detail being cut into the plate, which is then inked and wiped over, leaving ink only in the cuts, and finally an impression is taken by passing the plate through a printing press along with a dampened sheet of paper. In the nineteenth century copper engraving was challenged by engraving on steel, a process which did not call for new production methods but, because of the hardness of the metal, enabled many more impressions to be taken before the plate became worn.

Lithographic printing was introduced during the nineteenth century. It is a surface or *planographic* process depending, on the one hand, on the antipathy between grease and water and, on the other, on the affinity between one greasy substance and another. As the term *lithography* implies, the design, at the birth of the process, was drawn on a specially prepared stone with greasy ink. Impressions could then be taken from the stone. Nowadays metal, plastic and paper plates have superseded stone and the image is transferred photographically on to the plate from which copies can be run off at great speed on offset-litho printing machines.

Distinguishing an original printed map, i.e. an impression from the original block or plate, from a facsimile reproduction should not present a great problem for, in most cases, the name of the publisher of the facsimile will be clearly stated outside the border of the map. If any doubt exists it can be helpful to look for the *impression mark* outside the border of an original map. This is the indentation made by the printing press squeezing the printing plate into the paper. A modern litho-printed reproduction rarely features such a mark. There is no intent to make forgeries when producing facsimile maps and, indeed, such reproductions, if of good quality, can provide a useful service to serious students in making rare or unobtainable maps available for study purposes.

### The terminology of early maps

A knowledge of the technical terms used in connection with early maps is a helpful step towards fuller understanding. Such terms fall into various categories, the first of which refers to the state of the map.

An *impression* is a single example printed from a block or printing plate. Sometimes different impressions, on examination, reveal alterations to the plate. They are then said to be in different *states*, i.e. they are made from different states or conditions of the same block or plate. The total number of impressions taken from a plate at one time together constitutes an *issue*, while further sets of impressions taken from the plate are *reissues*. An *edition* consists of all issues and reissues printed from one state of a block or plate.

Various Latin terms and abbreviations are used on early maps to refer to the craftsmen engaged in their production:

(a) the cartographer, or person responsible for the surveying and for the preparation of the draft map for the engraver, may be indicated by one or other of the following: *descripsit, delineavit, delt., auctore*.

(b) the engraver is referred to in the following terms: *sculpsit, sculp., sc., fecit, caelavit, engr., incidit, incidente*.

(c) the printer or publisher is indicated by *excudit, excud., exc., sumptibus, ex officina*.

A variety of nomenclature has been used to denote a bound collection of maps. Ortelius used *Theatrum* in his *Theatrum Orbis Terrarum* (1570); John Norden used *Speculum* in the title of his proposed *Speculum Britanniae*; John Speed entitled his atlas *The Theatre of the Empire of Great Britaine* (1611). 'Theatre' like 'Speculum' and 'Theatrum' is used in the sense of a 'view' or 'display'. Lucas Jansz. Waghenaer used the word Spieghel in the title of his book of charts *De Spieghel der Zeevaerdt* (1584) or *Mariner's Mirror*. In 1585 Mercator employed the word *Atlas* for the first time and this has remained in common usage ever since.

Other terms seen occasionally are *geographer, cartographer, topographer* or *cosmographer*, all denoting a maker of maps; *hydrographer* (maker of marine charts); *illumineur* (map colourist).

## *Identifying an early map*

It is not always easy to date a map precisely for mapmakers often omitted the date of issue and, furthermore, even when the date was included, map plates were often used over and over again without alteration to the date; for example, a particular feature may be observed on a map which could not have existed at the date shown, thus clearly indicating revision of detail later than the date given on the map. One should be aware, therefore, that the printed date is not necessarily a reliable indication of the date of the topographical information on the map.

Fortunately, however, numerous carto-bibliographies are available to assist in identification. Thomas Chubb's *The Printed Maps in the Atlases of Great Britain and Ireland 1579-1870* was for a long time the standard authority but has been superseded in part by R. A. Skelton's definitive *County Atlases of the British Isles*. Owing to Skelton's untimely death this work covers only the period from 1579 to 1703 but Donald Hodson has taken matters further in *County Atlases of the British Isles Published after 1703*, volumes I and II. At county level many bibliographies are available, such as those by Sir H. G. Fordham and Harold Whitaker or the fine catalogue of Warwickshire maps by P. D. A. Harvey and Harry Thorpe. R. W. Shirley has published a definitive work, *The Mapping of the World,* which discusses world maps printed before 1700, and there are numerous carto-bibliographies covering the maps of individual countries. Of the latter Dr I. C. Koeman's remarkable five-volume *Atlantes Neerlandici* covers maps published in the Netherlands up to 1880. Where no detailed carto-bibliography is available it may be helpful to consult C. Verner's article 'The Identification and Designation of Variants in the Study of Early Printed Maps' (*Imago Mundi* volume XIX, 1965).

A map can usually be allocated to a specific period by a study of its style and ornamentation but more precise dating requires detailed examination of its physical and external characteristics as well as its topographical content. The paper on which the map is printed may provide clues and so may the state of wear on the printing plate. Other factors which should offer some guidance on dating fairly closely include an examination of the watermark, for a particular watermark will indicate the age and origin of the printing paper; the imprint should have useful evidence to the origins of the map; so too whether text is printed on the reverse of the map and, if so, the language in which it is written. The study of watermarks is an interesting, if complex, one and the interested reader is referred to Edward Heawood's paper 'The Use of Watermarks in Dating Old Maps and Documents', which can be found in two sources, *The Geographical Journal*, volume LXIII pages 391-400 (1924), and Raymond Lister's *How to Identify Old Maps and Globes* (Bell, 1965). In addition to the study of the physical characteristics of the map particular note should be taken of its topographical detail – roads, canals, railways and the extent of any settlement shown. In this context, however, it should be remembered that mapmakers occasionally anticipated the construction of a railway, for example, and so lines may appear on their maps which were not in existence at the time of publication.

# 1
# *Map design*

Any early map consists of two contrasting sets of features:
(a) the all-important topographical detail, lettering and symbolisation of the map itself;
(b) ancillary features such as a frame or border to hold the composition together, a title panel, scale of distance and decorative features such as illustrations of ships, flora and fauna.

These diverse features have to be blended together and here the skill of the engraver comes into its own. It is he who assembles all the separate items into a pleasing, graphic and balanced composition.

## *Topographical detail*
### *Seas and coasts*

An essential element of map design is that areas of sea and land should be clearly differentiated. Colour, using the traditional blue for water, offers an obvious solution but engravers have tried various techniques in an attempt to overcome the problem in black and white only. In woodcut maps, exemplified by the sixteenth-century maps of Sebastian Münster, simple wave patterns were engraved on sea areas. A little later, in maps by Abraham Ortelius for example, a stippled pattern of fine dots gave a distinguishing texture to sea areas. This was occasionally implemented by short horizontal lines drawn outwards from the coast. More refined wave patterns were devised later, such as those by Jodocus Hondius which resembled moiré or watered silk. During the late sixteenth and early seventeenth centuries it was common practice to fill sea areas with monsters or beautifully engraved sailing vessels. The Amsterdam mapmakers Blaeu and Jansson, however, often left sea areas blank except for the occasional ship and horizontal lining to accentuate the coastlines. The depiction of sailing craft of various kinds on early maps would make an interesting study just as Dr Wilma George studied the distribution of fauna in her fascinating book *Animals and Maps* (Secker & Warburg, 1969). *Form lines*, i.e. lines drawn parallel with the shore and gradually increasing in distance apart, were used to emphasise coastlines in the eighteenth century and this practice reached a peak of perfection in early Ordnance Survey maps.

### *Mountains and hills*

The depiction of relief has always posed problems for the mapmaker in that, ideally, heights of hills have to be accurately

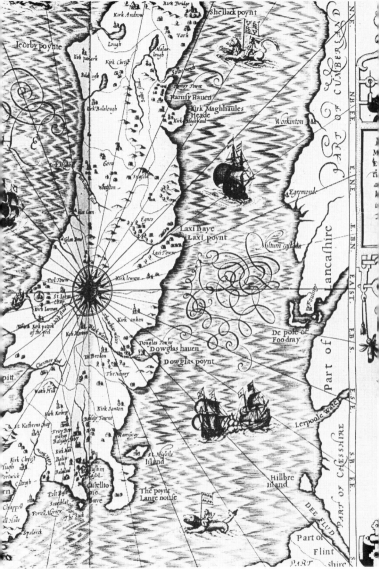

*Extravagant 'swash' lettering, sailing vessels, sea creatures, a compass rose and the moiré pattern on the sea areas are the main features of this rather elongated map of the Isle of Man from Speed's 'Theatre of the Empire of Great Britaine' (1611). Courtesy: University of Liverpool (H.17.2).*

shown as well as the length, breadth and shape of the hills. On a flat sheet of paper this is a very difficult problem. On medieval manuscript maps hills were crudely drawn in profile with shading on the sides to add substance. Early engraved maps such as the county maps of Christopher Saxton and John Speed featured hills resembling sugar loaves, shaded to one side, with no attempt at any consistent vertical scale but some effort at showing relative heights. Blaeu and his contemporaries were no nearer to a solution in the mid seventeenth century, merely engraving smaller hills and more of them. Pictorial representation continued towards the end of the seventeenth century when *hill shading*, i.e. lines drawn down the slopes, was employed in an effort to show hills in plan. This was a significant advance in that the length and breadth of a mountain or hill could be shown and, furthermore, steepness of slope could be suggested by thickening the lines of the hill shading. Precise indication of height, however, remained an insoluble problem.

In the eighteenth century ranges of hills were drawn in a form which has been likened to 'hairy caterpillars' but at the turn of the century *hachuring*, a more scientific development of hill shading, came into being, sometimes in conjunction with *spot heights*. The *contour* method, by which height or depth could at last be indicated effectively, was first used by a Dutchman, N. S. Cruquius, to chart a river bed in 1729, and in 1737 Philippe Buache depicted the depths of the English Channel by marine contours. On land maps, however, contours did not come into use until well into the nineteenth century.

*Woodland and parks*

The conventional representation of woodland has changed very little as it was customary from the time of the earliest manuscript maps to represent woodland and forest symbolically by means of trees stylistically drawn in elevation and coloured green. On engraved maps the trees were smaller and in greater numbers. Often they were given shadows to the east, which, together with the shading on the eastern slopes of hills, suggested the area of the map was lit from the west.

Saxton introduced a symbol for great parks on his English county maps in the form of a group of trees surrounded by a pale fence.

*Settlement*

Towns received pictorial treatment in elevation on medieval manuscript maps but since then there has been a gradual change, first to the bird's eye perspective view and later to depiction entirely in plan. The Bodleian Map of the British Isles (*c.*1360) features pictorial symbols for varying categories of town: ordinary towns are shown by cream-washed buildings with red tiled roofs; small monastic towns have buildings with spires; London receives its own individual treatment, its buildings having blue leaded roofs, painted timber beams, spires, crosses and battlements.

During the sixteenth century mapmakers tried to depict towns partly in plan and partly in elevation by raising their viewpoint and drawing in bird's eye perspective. This treatment, which can be very effective, is well seen in some of the plans in Braun and Hogenberg's *Civitates Orbis Terrarum* (1572-1617). It is a particularly useful way of graphically illustrating the unique character and architecture of a town.

On small-scale maps pictorial symbols composed of a group of buildings showed whether a town had fortifications and indicated its relative size by the number of buildings in the group. Following the decline in importance of the medieval castle, it was superseded on maps by the church as the symbol representing a town or

*Mercator's fine calligraphy is well demonstrated in this map of north-east Italy (c.1600). Hills are shaded on the east, rivers are prominent and towns are usually symbolised by a small circle enclosing a small dot.*

village. One map which is particularly remarkable for its pictorial treatment of village churches is Philip Symonson's superb county map of Kent (1596). On many early engraved maps which have been hand-coloured the delicate engraving of town symbols was obscured by a tendency to colour them thickly in red, a practice which persisted until the late eighteenth century.

From the early days of mapmaking the circle has been associated with settlement and from 1520 it was used in conjunction with church towers or other buildings to symbolise towns and cities, the circle being placed as an indication of the town centre and the point from which distances should be measured.

German mapmakers of the mid sixteenth century, such as Philipp Apian, introduced numerous symbols for settlement which were explained in a table of conventional signs or *legend*. Similar explanatory legends were introduced into Britain by William Smith and John Norden.

John Speed included inset plans of county towns on the county maps in his *Theatre of the Empire of Great Britaine* (1611) and in so doing produced the first extensive set of British town plans. Marginal town plans and views were introduced into the borders of maps by Ortelius, Blaeu, Visscher and others. These not only introduced a decorative element but presented additional information to the detail on the maps themselves.

The period from 1675 to 1740 was one of transition when scientifically constructed large-scale plans, such as the superb plan of London by Ogilby and Morgan (1677), appeared at the same time as traditional bird's eye views and elevations. On small-scale maps the larger towns were drawn in plan by means of blocks of buildings through which white roads threaded their way. Smaller towns and villages were symbolised by rows of houses drawn in perspective along the road sides.

After 1740 the practice of drawing settlements in plan became much more popular and with the advent of the Ordnance Survey one inch to one mile maps in the early nineteenth century it became the standard technique.

## *Ancillary features*
### *The cartouche*

Certain components of map design do not form any part of the information being presented but are ancillary to it. On early maps the most prominent of such features is the *cartouche*, a panel, often extravagantly ornamented, which serves to contain a title, legend or dedication.

On early engraved maps the title was sometimes placed in the upper margin while in the early sixteenth century it was often

*An ornamental cartouche from the Lancashire map in Saxton's 'Atlas of England and Wales' (1579).*

written in a flying scroll. Italians introduced the cartouche displaying title and relevant information concerning the map. On early woodcut maps the design was necessarily simple for the woodcut technique was not well suited to intricate ornamentation. Copper engraving, however, allowed the craftsman to develop the ornament of the cartouche, often in a characteristic strapwork design resembling lengths of interwoven leather with curling ends. Designs of this kind can be seen on many maps by Saxton and Speed. Another popular cartouche design in the sixteenth and early seventeenth centuries resembled a carved wooden framework with curling projections supporting the title panel. From the late sixteenth to the mid seventeenth century, a period when the Dutch held supremacy in cartography, cartouche design reflected the influence of pattern books of Renaissance sculpture, wood carving, jewellery, stone and plaster work. Designs were further influenced by hammerbeam roofing in Gothic churches and houses. Additional embellishments of fish, fruit and flowers were common. After *c.*1580 smaller, equally ornate cartouches were introduced to house the linear distance scale or the dedication. In the early seventeenth century the pseudo-wooden frame gradually disappeared and strapwork was reintroduced, though now in a form more reminiscent of plasterwork than of leather. In the middle of the century scenes of local life were common and may be seen to advantage on many maps by the Blaeu family.

The baroque style of ornamentation exerted a strong influence on map design with cartouches incorporating masses of flowers and fruit, human figures, putti, animals and architectural detail. The wood carvings of Grinling Gibbons and painted ceilings by Italian artists such as Verrio also played their part in influencing map ornamentation.

Rococo succeeded baroque in the mid eighteenth century and is splendidly seen in the county maps of Emanuel Bowen. The style was light and elegant with ornamentation derived from the drawing room – cartouches resembling rococo mirrors or Chippendale chair backs. Influence was also drawn from the countryside: title panels, for instance, often consisted of stone slabs around which country folk displayed farm implements, produce and animals.

The Romantic movement in England left its mark on map design in the portrayal of classical ruins – pillars often framing a title against a background landscape. Many one inch to one mile county maps published during the eighteenth century had superb cartouches or vignetted scenes of landscape and buildings. The two splendid series of county maps by John Cary and Charles Smith, however, eschewed decoration, their titles being housed within the simplest panels. The Old Series one-inch sheets of the Ordnance Survey had no decoration whatsoever.

*The border or frame*

Irregularly shaped maps have been traditionally held together by enclosing them within a rectangular frame, a convention which left unwanted space between the area of the map itself and the frame. The engraver could use his imagination and skills in design to decorate such spaces in one way or another. Ortelius, in the late sixteenth century, filled in the corners of some of his maps with elegant designs which appear to have been derived from metalwork while Emanuel Bowen, in the eighteenth century, used the spaces to great advantage by filling them with long descriptive notes about the area depicted on the map itself.

Sixteenth-century Italian maps had plain borders, sometimes graduated in degrees of latitude and longitude, a device commonly

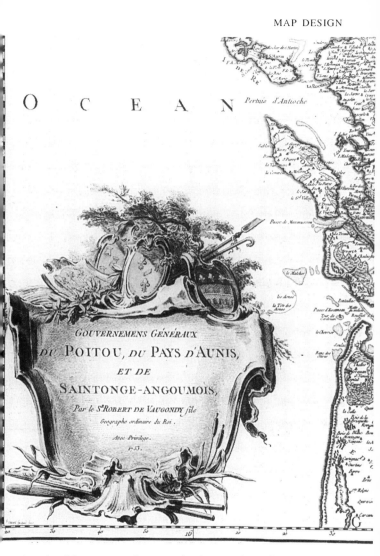

*A splendid ornamental cartouche from Robert de Vaugondy's map of a part of western France (1753).*

*Heraldry, an ornamental border, 'swash' lettering, academic figures and the royal arms decorate this section of Speed's beautiful Cambridgeshire map in his 'Theatre of the Empire of Great Britaine' (1611). Courtesy: University of Liverpool (H.17.2).*

used today. Maps from the Low Countries had patterned borders resembling picture frames. Ortelius, Blaeu and Visscher, among others, incorporated local scenes, figures, representation of the elements and particularly small plans and views of towns in map borders known as *cartes à figures* or 'figured borders'. One particularly attractive and colourful idea was to introduce heraldic shields into the border, either in regular fashion as in Speed's county map of Cambridgeshire, or interlaced as in Blaeu's map of Piedmont. The practice of using heraldic shields reached its zenith when John Harris included 152 shields in the border of his map of Kent (1719).

The borders of early Ordnance Survey one inch to one mile maps are faintly reminiscent of the piano keyboard, an idea which seems to have influenced county mapmakers – C. and J. Greenwood, for example – who used variations on this theme.

*The linear distance scale*

A linear scale of distance plays a vital functional role on any map. Without it a map is almost meaningless. In the past, however, it also served as a decorative feature. Through the centuries it has been common practice to incorporate a pair of dividers into the scale design, sometimes held by small naked cherubs, who may also wield surveying chains and instruments. Before the legal establishment of the statute mile of 1760 yards in 1593 various local or 'customary' miles were in use. Indeed, they remained in use for over a century afterwards: on Robert Morden's county maps, for instance, scales representing 'great', 'middle' and 'small' miles are included while on some European maps national scales featuring 'German' or 'Italian' distances are to be seen. The ultimate confusion to the map reader comes with Julien's map of France (1651) on which there are no less than twenty different scales of distance!

*Orientation*

It is common practice today to print maps so that north is at the top of the sheet or page but there is no logical reason for doing so, except perhaps to establish a standard convention. Early medieval mapmakers set east to the top in deference to the holy places of the Orient – hence the term 'orientation' and the modern sport of 'orienteering'. The practice of orienting maps to the north was established by Italian and Catalan makers of nautical charts but in the late eighteenth and early nineteenth centuries maps were occasionally given a different orientation, often to enable them to fit the prescribed area of the printed page – in John Cary's *Traveller's Companion*, for example, the Cheshire map is engraved with west at the top – or to display the area under consideration to greatest advantage.

## Colouring

Early engraved maps were invariably printed in black and white with hand colouring added at an extra charge for individual customers. Map colouring was a specialised, highly respected profession – Ortelius, in the early stages of his career, was a map colourist and in the seventeenth century the profession was so highly regarded that Nicholas Berey was granted the resounding title of *enlumineur de la reine*.

In the sixteenth and seventeenth centuries brilliant hand colouring was lavished on the more decorative parts of maps with the topographical detail receiving somewhat lighter treatment. Certain conventions in colouring were established: hills, brown or green; woodland, green; rivers and seas, blue; settlements, red. Boundaries were normally coloured in outline with a narrow band of colour but the eighteenth-century Germans Homann and Seutter brushed a colour wash over whole provinces, a practice which tended to give their work a rather dull, heavy appearance. It is difficult today, even for an expert, to establish just when a map has been coloured, for the profession of map colourist still exists and it is not uncommon for genuine early engraved maps to receive modern hand colouring. The collector should be aware that when he sees the term 'contemporary' applied to map colouring it will almost certainly mean contemporary with the printing of the map and not present-day. A modern litho-printed reproduction can be fairly easily distinguished from a hand-coloured original if each is examined through a magnifying glass. The hand colouring will be seen as solid areas of colour while the colour printing will appear as multitudinous tiny dots due to the use of fine dot screens in the printing process. Several accounts of map colouring survive, the most detailed being in John Smith's *The Art of Painting in Oyl* (1701). A lengthy extract from this work which deals with the colouring of maps appears in Raymond Lister's *How to Identify Old Maps and Globes* (Bell, 1965).

## Calligraphy

The primary requirements of lettering for cartography are legibility, perceptibility and suitability so that, in turn, it can clearly be read with the naked eye, stands out well from the background and suits the process by which the map is printed. Failure to comply with these requirements may ruin an otherwise excellent piece of mapwork. Early wood engravers favoured the

Germanic *Gothic* or *black-letter*, but with the greater flexibility allowed by copper engraving *Roman* and smoothly flowing *italic* alphabets became common in the sixteenth century. The great Flemish cartographer Gerardus Mercator, needing a clear type of lettering for his map of both hemispheres of the globe in 1538, adopted his own italic script and wrote a treatise about it in which he studied such matters as the cutting of the quill pen, the holding of the pen and the composition and formation of minuscules and capitals. Illustrations from this treatise can be found in *Gerardus Mercator, Cartographer and Writing Master* (Werner Renckhoff KG, Duisburg, 1962). Apart from the beautiful scripts used in the majority of Flemish and Dutch maps, a flamboyant style known as swash, which had sweeping tails and flourishes to the letters, was often used to fill up unwanted spaces such as empty areas of sea.

# 2
# The origins and early development of mapmaking

How and where maps were first made is something about which we can only surmise. We do know, however, that primitive peoples possess an inborn ability to make rudimentary maps of their surroundings and this has led to the assumption that the making of simple sketch maps is older than writing and that maps, therefore, are older than written history. The earliest cartographical representation of any kind that we know of is the famous topographical village plan of Bedolina, a plan incised in a rock face in the Val Camonica near Capo di Ponte in northern Italy. This plan includes lively illustrations of huts, fields, boundary walls, streams and canals. It dates from the bronze age. The earliest extant map of a portable nature, however, is inscribed on a small clay tablet found at Gar Sur, 200 miles (320 km) north of Babylon. Dating from approximately 3800 BC, it shows a river, probably the Euphrates, flowing out through a delta and flanked by two mountain ranges which are depicted in a style which resembles fish scales. The Babylonians achieved the primary element of mapmaking – that of establishing the position of any place so that it could be located at any time – for they divided the circle of the sky into 360 degrees and the day into hours, minutes and seconds, thus enabling any point on the earth's surface to be plotted in relation to the stars.

Concrete evidence of Egyptian contributions to the early evolution of mapmaking is sparse though we do know that land was measured and recorded for taxation purposes, inscriptions on the tombs of prominent citizens bearing records of such surveys. A certain amount is known about the methods employed in making the surveys – cords and rods being used in linear measurements, with knots placed at intervals in the cords to mark off units of length.

We are indebted to the Greeks, however, for the true foundations of scientific mapmaking. Eratosthenes, accepting the theory of a spherical world, calculated a remarkably accurate figure for its circumference but a later astronomer, Posidonius, made new, erroneous calculations which were 7000 miles (11,000 km) too low. These later figures were accepted and exerted an unfortunate influence on mapmaking for centuries. The greatest Greek geographer was Claudius Ptolemy (AD 90 to 168), whose famous *Geographia* dealt with the construction of globes and map projections as well as providing a list of some eight thousand places with their latitudes and longitudes. The world could now be fitted into a scientific framework to which new discoveries could be added as they were made. There were, however, errors in Ptolemy's figures. Because he used the erroneous calculations of Posidonius, he underestimated the earth's size. He believed that Asia and Europe together occupied over half the circumference of the globe and calculated the length of the Mediterranean to be 62° instead of its correct 42°, an error which persisted on maps derived from his data until 1700. *Geographia* includes twenty-six regional maps and a world map in what is known as the A recension while a group of sixty-seven maps of smaller areas forms the B recension. As there are no surviving manuscript maps based on Ptolemy earlier than the twelfth century, it is not known whether Ptolemy drew maps himself or whether they had been merely ascribed to him on his reputation as a geographer. *Geographia* was lost to the western world for centuries, though it exerted an influence on Islamic geography, and was not brought back to Europe until the fifteenth century, when it played a major part in furthering a great renaissance of classical cartography.

The Romans made surprisingly little contribution to cartographic progress, their primary concern being with surveys to assist in the administration and military requirements of their widely spread empire. One such practical map is the so-called *Peutinger Table*, an eleventh- or twelfth-century copy of a route map originally made in the first century AD and since much revised. The late copy was located in 1507 by Konrad Celtis and bequeathed to an Augsburg collector, Konrad A. Peutinger, after whom it is now named. Other examples which illustrate wider thinking by the Romans about cartography are to be seen in the small schematic map/diagrams which are found in medieval editions of certain scholarly classical texts such as those of Macrobius and Sallust. It is also believed that a world map based on military road surveys within the Roman Empire was made by Marcus Vipsanius Agrippa (63 BC to 12 BC) and there has been speculation that the *Peutinger Table* could be a modified version of Agrippa's map.

## *Islamic cartography*

When the Roman Empire was dissolved western European cartography entered a period of decline in which scant regard was paid to early scholarship. In the Islamic world, however, Arab scholars skilled in the sciences of astronomy, mathematics and geometry had access to manuscripts of Ptolemy's *Geographia* and in the eighth century AD a translation into Arabic was made. Among notable Arab accomplishments were the determination of the latitude and longitude of places by astronomical observation and the reduction of Ptolemy's overestimated length of the Mediterranean Sea to the correct 42°. Religious treatises were illustrated by small circular maps centred on Mecca but the outstanding achievement was a world map by al-Idrisi, an Arab cartographer at the court of the Norman King Roger of Sicily, in which he divided the world into seven climatic zones, a theory based on Greek science and developed in the Islamic world.

## The medieval period

Following the collapse of the Roman Empire the spread of Christianity led to the appearance of new maps which were centred on Jerusalem. Monastic writings were often illustrated with maps known as *T-O* or *T in O* maps. These were circular in shape with east to the top and Jerusalem at the centre. The ocean flowed around the circumference of the circle to form the O while the T, placed inside the O, divided the map into three parts. The vertical stroke of the T was formed by the Mediterranean Sea and the horizontal bar consisted of a line from the river Don to the Nile. Such medieval maps were produced in great numbers, usually simple in form but in some cases bearing a wealth of detail, elaborate ornamentation and brilliant colouring. They gave graphic expression to the medieval world view as declaimed in the writings of Isidore, a seventh-century Bishop of Seville, who wrote as follows: 'the earth (Orbis) was named from its roundness...Europe and Africa were made in two parts because the great sea (called the Mediterranean) enters from the ocean between them and cuts them in half.'

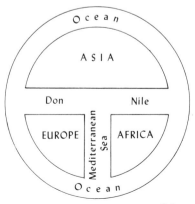

*A schematic diagram of the T-O or T in O world map principle.*

Not all medieval world maps were small book illustrations: one of the finest is preserved in Hereford Cathedral and was made c.1300 by Richard of Haldingham. Measuring over 5 feet (1.5 metres) in diameter, this colourful circular map illustrates the biblical world, centred on Jerusalem, with the figure of Christ presiding at the top (or east). It is richly decorated with detail from biblical lore, medieval histories and bestiaries. Representation of the British Isles is extremely poor for they appear at the very edge of the map and have been bent round to fit into the circle, resulting in a highly distorted shape, on which, nevertheless, some new place-names are included. The Ebstorf map of the same period was even larger and more magnificent, measuring over 13 feet (4 metres) in diameter. It was built round the figure of Christ on a fairly standard T-O pattern with a richly gilded Jerusalem in the centre. The map was formerly preserved at a monastery in Germany but was regrettably destroyed by bombing during the Second World War. Fortunately reproductions of the map are available.

## Matthew Paris

Among the finest maps of the early middle ages were the four of Great Britain made by Matthew Paris, a monk of St Albans c.1250, whose books included numerous illustrations, amongst them a world map, a map of Palestine and the four of Great Britain. Although crude in detail, the maps present a readily recognisable portrait of the country and are constructed around the pilgrim route from the north to Dover. The stations along this route are laid down along the central vertical axis of each map and, in order to conform to this axial route, Matthew had inevitably to resort to a certain amount of distortion: for instance he places the Thames estuary on the south coast. Nevertheless, he clearly recognised some of the fundamental principles of mapmaking, notably the necessity of drawing to a uniform scale, and, furthermore, he included a great deal of detail, naming over 250 places as well as rivers and a number of hills.

## The Gough or Bodleian Map

First described by Richard Gough in 1780 and now in the care of the Bodleian Library, Oxford (hence the alternative names), this remarkably fine map was made c.1360 and even a casual glance reveals the tremendous advance it represents. A map of the British Isles, 3 feet 9$^{1}/_{2}$ inches by 1 foot 10 inches (1156 mm by 559mm), it was made on two joined skins of vellum and, although the north-south extent is exaggerated, the general outline is remarkably good. Rivers are prominently shown, presumably due to their importance in communications; mountains are poorly depicted;

*One of four maps of Great Britain by the monk of St Albans, Matthew Paris, showing the pilgrim route from the north to Dover (c.1250). By permission of the British Library (Claudius D.vi.f.12v).*

*Supremely artistic ornamentation and elegant calligraphy are seen in this detail of a manuscript chart attributed to the Homem family and dated c.1569. Courtesy: University of Liverpool (Ms.F.4.3).*

but, to quote Richard Gough, 'the greatest merit of this map is, that it may justly boast itself the first among us wherein the roads and distances are laid down'. Roads are shown as straight lines which join the pictorial town symbols. Distances, which are astonishingly accurate, are given in Roman figures. This remarkable map exerted an influence on the mapping of Britain for over two centuries.

## Mappae Mundi

The finest example of monastic mapmaking was a circular world map made by Fra Mauro, a monk of Murano, an island in the Venetian lagoon. Over 6 feet (1.8 metres) in diameter, the map contained a vast amount of detail. Made in 1457-9, the Asiatic part of the map was largely based on the writings of Marco Polo. Other sections of the map owe something to contemporary nautical charts, something to Ptolemy and something to travellers' itineraries. A break with ecclesiastical tradition is made in that the map is oriented to the south, rather than the east, and that the map is not centred on Jerusalem. Indeed Fra Mauro's map can be said to mark the end of theologically based mapmaking and the beginning of an era of scientific cartography.

Almost fifty years later, in 1500, a great manuscript map of the world was made by Juan de la Cosa, a seaman on the first voyage of Columbus, whose map was executed in the style of the contemporary portolan charts (see chapter 9). It is a highly decorative map with a wealth of coastal detail and includes some interior detail. The demarcation line resulting from the Treaty of Tordesillas in 1494 indicates the division between Spanish and Portuguese spheres of influence in the Americas and, indeed, Juan de la Cosa's map is the earliest documentary graphic illustration of the discovery of the New World. The continuing influence of Ptolemy is seen in the poor depiction of India and south-east Asia but the discoveries made by Portuguese navigators resulted in de la Cosa being able to provide a greatly improved view of the African continent.

# 3
# The printed map

The period around 1500 was one of exceptional significance to cartographical development owing to three important factors which revolutionised thinking about geography and cartography, introduced a great amount of new data which had to be incorporated into the content of maps, and enormously facilitated the dissemination of knowledge by making maps readily available to a wider public rather than a highly privileged few.

The first of these three factors was the reintroduction into Europe of manuscripts of Ptolemy's *Geographia* after being lost to the west for centuries, during which time it had exerted an influence on Islamic cartography. The manuscripts were speedily translated into Latin and their arrival stimulated scholars into deserting theologically based mapmaking for a welcome return to the scientific approaches of the classical world.

The content of contemporary maps was wholly revolutionised by the second of the three stimuli: this was the age of the great discoveries when explorers were searching out in all directions and navigators such as Vasco da Gama, Cabot and Columbus were returning from their questing voyages with a great wealth of new information which had to be added to contemporary maps.

Arguably the most significant of the three factors was the application of the newly developed craft of printing to map production. Printing had been applied to Chinese maps as early as the twelfth century but did not penetrate into Europe until the late fifteenth century, when it produced the greatest watershed in cartographic history, matched only perhaps by the introduction of automated processes in the twentieth century. The introduction of printing, firstly from wood blocks and later from engraved copper sheets, facilitated the publication of a succession of printed editions of Ptolemy's *Geographia* in which maps carrying the geographical knowledge of Ptolemy from centuries earlier were being reproduced by the most up-to-date technology. A rethinking of the concepts of Ptolemy was essential and world mapmakers at the outset of the sixteenth century attempted to reconcile Ptolemaic geography with the growing wealth of new data.

A prime requisite of the printing process was the provision of a light durable material which would accept ink and stand up to the rigours of the printing press. Paper was an ideal medium and, fortunately, was available. Used in China for book printing as early as the ninth century AD, the papermaking technique spread slowly

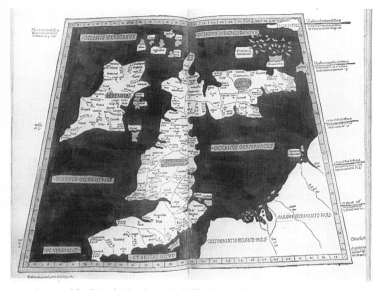

*A map of the British Isles from the 1482 edition of Ptolemy's 'Geographia', printed in Ulm. The curious east-west alignment of Scotland is a striking feature. Courtesy: University of Liverpool (E.P.A. 4.15).*

westwards, reaching Spain in the tenth century, France in the twelfth, Germany in the fourteenth and England in the fifteenth.

The woodcut technique of printing, as mentioned earlier, is a relief method of printing in which those areas not to be printed are cut away, leaving the design in relief. The earliest printed woodcut map was a small diagrammatic world map which appeared as an illustration in a 1472 edition of the *Etymologiae* of the seventh-century Bishop Isidore of Seville. Woodcut maps appeared in several printed editions of Ptolemy, a particularly attractive set illustrating the 1482 Ulm edition of *Geographia*. Encyclopaedic works such as the *Cosmographia* of Sebastian Münster and Peter Apian also included woodcut illustrations. Two attempts at colour printing illustrate the ambition of early cartographers to improve techniques of presentation and so make maps more efficient as a means of communication. The first of these was made by Bernard Sylvanus in his Venice edition of Ptolemy (1511): in this case there were probably two printings, one in red, the second in black, so that a map was produced in which most of the detail was in black but some names were printed in red. The second attempt, made by

Martin Waldseemüller in his Strasbourg edition of Ptolemy (1513), was more ambitious in that it attempted a three-colour printing. It was, unfortunately, less successful in that colour registration was not good and the colours themselves were inconsistent in quality.

The woodcut technique had severe limitations in that linework tended to be rather crude and any kind of tone or small symbol was difficult to reproduce. These problems were overcome to a great extent with the introduction of printing from engraved copper plates. This technique, in which the design is incised into the plate, allowed finer detail to be produced, neater symbolisation and linework, and more elegant styles of lettering. Alterations were easier and the copper plates could be much larger than the wood blocks had been so that the process was ideally suited to the production of fairly large single-sheet maps or to the folio sheets of an atlas.

### The early German school

As in other branches of art, mapmaking has tended to fall into national schools. In the late fifteenth and early sixteenth centuries the centres of geographical learning were in the southern German cities of Augsburg and Nuremberg. Here, felicitously, the craft of wood engraving flourished, with famed artists such as Holbein and Dürer at work. In Nuremberg in 1493 Hartmann Schedel produced his monumental *Nuremberg Chronicle* with many maps, town views and portraits engraved by Dürer's master, Michael Wohlgemut. Nuremberg was famous for fine globes, including that by Martin Behaim (1492) which can be seen in the city's National Germanic Museum. Primitive road maps were also produced, including the first road map in printed form, a *Romweg* or guide for pilgrims journeying to Rome made *c.*1500 by Erhard Etzlaub.

Woodcut editions of Ptolemy were published in Ulm and Strasbourg and in 1528 Sebastian Münster planned a composite atlas under his own editorship for which he invited German geographers to send him maps of their own provinces. Much of the resulting material appeared in his 1540 edition of Ptolemy and his own *Cosmographia* (1544).

Two other German scholars working on cartography in the first half of the sixteenth century were the astronomer and mathematician Peter Apian of Ingolstadt, who published numerous cartographical works including a world map on a heart-shaped projection, and his son, Philipp, whose best-known work is a magnificent large-scale map of Bavaria (1563).

Another great German school of geography and cartography was based in Cologne. The finest work to be produced there was the celebrated city atlas *Civitates Orbis Terrarum* (1573-1618). This was a six-volume work devoted to plans and views of the towns

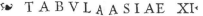

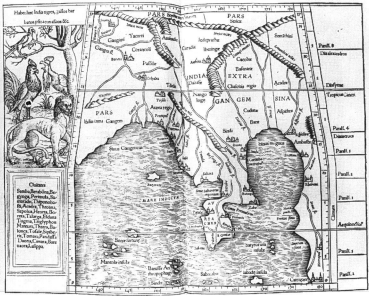

*A map of part of southern Asia showing the mouths of the Ganges with illustrations of animals and birds in the panel on the left. From Sebastian Münster's edition of Ptolemy's 'Geographia' (Basle, 1540). Courtesy: University of Liverpool (Ryl.N.2.14).*

and cities of Europe and prepared by Georg Braun and the engraver Frans Hogenberg. The colourful illustrations have much to tell us about the urban scene, featuring scenes of local life with figures in the local costume of the day.

### *The Italian school*

Credit for the revival of interest in Ptolemy's classic *Geographia* must go to Italian scholars. Early editions which included copper-engraved maps were printed in Bologna (1477), Rome (1478), Florence (1482) and Rome again (1490). These editions were excellent examples of craftsmanship and in the early sixteenth century the Italian Renaissance was at its peak – Italian craftsmen were supreme and so, too, were Italian mapmakers.

The map trade flourished in Rome and Venice, where men such as Lafreri, Bertelli and Camocio may well be termed 'publishers' for they combined the skills of cartography, engraving, printing, publishing and mapselling. The finest of the Italian school of cartography was Jacopo Gastaldi, whose prolific output included the maps for the 1548 Venice edition of Ptolemy. Italian publishers may be credited with producing the prototype of a modern atlas for they assembled in one volume, to order, collections of maps put together from their stock. Sixty to seventy of this type of 'atlas' survive. The maps are arranged in Ptolemy's system of precedence. These Italian atlases, of which no two are alike either in the selection or the number of maps included, have been termed 'Lafreri atlases'.

Among later Italian work, the atlas of sea charts *Arcano del Mare* (1646-7) by Sir Robert Dudley, an Englishman who settled in Florence, stands out both for its geographical content and for the quality of the engraving by Antonio Francesco Lucini. Towards the end of the seventeenth century the Venetian cartographer Vincenzo Maria Coronelli was responsible for several interesting terrestrial and celestial globes varying in diameter from 3 inches (76 mm) to 15 feet (4.5 metres). Coronelli founded the first geographical society, *Gli Argonauti*, in Venice in 1680 and gathered together his immense cartographic output in the twelve-volume *Atlante Veneto* (1697-1701).

Well before this time, however, Italian influence on map production had declined, notably after 1570 when Abraham Ortelius published the first edition of his atlas, *Theatrum Orbis Terrarum*. From this point cartographic supremacy passed to the Low Countries and a period of mapmaking commenced in which the new maps were unsurpassed for accuracy (given the geographical knowledge of the time), elegance and richness of ornamentation.

## Belgium and Holland

At first cartographic output was centred on Flanders, and Antwerp in particular. In this city the arts were flourishing and outstanding maps and atlases were printed at the renowned printing house of Christopher Plantin (open to visitors today and displaying many of the fine productions of the house as well as wood blocks, copper plates, the shop where maps and atlases were sold, the original printing presses, sets of type, maps and globes etc). Antwerp was one of the major places in Europe for the production of fine-quality copper plates. Here, too, the great cartographer Abraham Ortelius was born. Ortelius is best known for his *Theatrum Orbis Terrarum* (1573), a magnificent atlas in which he assembled maps of the regions of the world which were based on contemporary information from the most reliable sources he could find. Ortelius was a cartographic editor who had his maps uniformly engraved in the same style and at a uniform size. In so doing he enabled the world to be presented graphically in one volume in far greater detail than had heretofore been possible on the traditional single world map. Many

*An interesting detail from G. B. Ramusio's map of Brazil in 'Delle Navigazioni e Viaggi' (Venice, 1556). West is to the top of the map and in the south Pernanbue (Pernambuco) and the Cabo de Sao Roque are clearly identified. While topographical detail is sparse there are revealing details of native life. Courtesy: University of Liverpool (Ryl.N.s.24-6).*

34

*Russia, a map from 'Theatrum Orbis Terrarum' (1570) by Abraham Ortelius. It is based on a famed map of 1562 by Anthony Jenkinson, the first English ambassador to Russia, who made a remarkable journey south to Bukhara in 1558. Courtesy: University of Liverpool (Ryl.N.2.14).*

of the maps were engraved by Frans Hogenberg and *Theatrum* was an immediate success, being translated into several languages and running into forty-two editions, the final one being issued in 1612.

Probably the best-known name in early cartography is that of Gerardus Mercator, a man of diverse talents ranging from engraving, instrument making and surveying to the manufacture of globes. A distinguished geographer and a mapmaker of outstanding ability, Mercator, born in Rupelmonde near Antwerp in 1512, was the inventor of the great map projection which bears his name and used the term 'atlas' for the first time to denote a bound set of maps. Mercator studied in Louvain under Gemma Frisius. Here he became established as an instrument maker and cartographer, drawing and engraving a map of Palestine (1537), a four-sheet map of Flanders (1538), a world map (1538) and a terrestrial globe (1541). In 1544 he was arrested on a charge of heresy but was cleared. Nevertheless

*Osnaburg and Münster from the English edition of 'Theatrum Orbis Terrarum' (London, 1606) by Ortelius. The cartouche is typical Renaissance strapwork and a clear key is provided to the symbols used.*

he moved to Duisburg in 1552, believing that in Germany there would be a more tolerant attitude to religious questions. From Duisburg he maintained cordial relations with like-minded scholars worldwide, particularly with his friend Ortelius. He developed his famed cylindrical projection in which all lines of latitude are parallel to the equator and those of longitude are perpendicular to it, enabling navigators to steer a course by straight lines without a continual adjustment of compass readings. In 1569 Mercator's great world map, in eighteen sheets and presented on his new projection, was published and in 1585 the first part of his *Atlas* appeared, to be followed by Part II in 1590 and Part III in 1595, the last part being a posthumous publication. The son of Gerardus, Rumold Mercator, was also a distinguished mapmaker and brought out a composite edition of Parts I, II and III of the Mercator *Atlas* in 1595. A second edition followed in 1602.

Mercator was followed by a succession of illustrious cartographers including his sons, Rumold and Arnold, and Arnold's sons, Gerard, John and Michael. The Mercator publishing business, however, was taken over by the engraver and publisher Jodocus Hondius, who issued expanded editions of Mercator's *Atlas* in Amsterdam from 1606. An engraver of unrivalled quality, Jodocus was responsible for engraving the plates for John Speed's first set of county maps in *The Theatre of the Empire of Great Britaine* (1611). After his death in 1611 his son, Henricus, took charge of the business and issued further editions of the Mercator *Atlas*.

In the early and middle years of the seventeenth century Amsterdam took over Antwerp's place as the prime focus of mapmaking in Europe. Here the rival publishing houses of Blaeu and Jansson were producing maps and atlases of incomparable beauty and elegance. Willem Janszoon Blaeu compiled a great map of the world – *Nova Totius Terrarum Orbis Tabula* – on twenty sheets in 1648. This production has been described as 'highest expression of Dutch cartographical art' (F. C. Wieder, *Monumenta Cartographica*, 1925-34). Other notable Blaeu publications include *Het Licht der Zeevaerdt* or *Light of Navigation* (1608), with forty-two sea charts; *Der Zeespiegel* (1623), including 111 charts; an atlas entitled *Theatrum Orbis Terrarum sive Atlas Novus* (1635-55), of which only two volumes had appeared at the time of W. J. Blaeu's death in 1638. The business was carried on by his sons, Joan and Cornelis, and the six-volume *Atlas Novus* was completed in 1655. Cornelis died in 1648 and Joan carried on alone, producing a truly great atlas, probably the finest ever, the *Atlas Maior* or *Grand Atlas* in eleven volumes (one edition with French text had twelve volumes), with three thousand folio pages of text and approximately six hundred map plates. Amazingly, while this gigantic project was under way Joan Blaeu was also engaged in the preparation of his marvellous town atlases of Italy, comprising 148 engravings and over seven hundred text pages. During the seventeenth century luxury editions in special artistic bindings were traditionally presented to important visitors to the Netherlands.

Amsterdam, in the late sixteenth and seventeenth centuries, was at its height as a mercantile power and there was an increasing demand for better and more up-to-date nautical charts. The commercial production of marine charts, sea atlases and pilot books, therefore, was a flourishing trade with important publishers such as Jacob Colom, Pieter Goos, Hendrick Doncker and Lucas Waghenaer making a formidable list of practicioners. Johannes van Keulen founded a most important printing house in Amsterdam which produced some of the finest sea atlases of the time.

### Early cartography in France

The greatest French cartographer of the sixteenth century was Oronce Finé (1494-1555), who was especially interested in the techniques of survey, in the development of improved surveying instruments and in compiling lunar tables for the determination of latitude. His cartographical output included a heart-shaped world map (1519), a world map on a double heart-shaped projection (1531), other world maps in 1536 and 1544 and a large woodcut map of France (1525).

In 1594 Maurice Bougereau issued *Le Théâtre François*, a work which contained general maps together with fifteen maps of French provinces. As such it constituted the first national atlas of France and may be said to lay the foundation of the cartography of the French provinces which was to culminate in the splendid atlas (1757) of Robert de Vaugondy. However, it was the work of Nicolas Sanson of Abbeville (1600-67) which truly led to the greatest period of French cartography when what has come to be known as the 'French School' flourished. Sanson was succeeded by his sons, Adrien and Guillaume, and later by various descendants who carried on an important cartographic dynasty which left for posterity a great number of fine maps and atlases. The Sanson dynasty was followed by Alexis Hubert Jaillot (*c*.1632-1712), who succeeded to many of the Sanson publications. Jaillot's maps were outstanding for their wealth of colour and ornament, examples of which Sir George Fordham[1] describes as the 'final glory' of the art of hand-colouring maps. Among the most notable of Jaillot's works are his *Atlas Nouveau* (1689) based, like much of his output, on the work of the Sansons, and *Le Neptune Françoys* (1693), a superb atlas of sea charts.

At the beginning of the eighteenth century the most prominent

French cartographer was Guillaume De l'Isle (1678-1726), who in 1718 was made Premier Géographe du Roi. Other outstanding exponents of mapmaking included Jean Baptiste Bourguignon d'Anville (1697-1782), Philippe Buache (1700-73), who is remembered for his use of marine contours or *isobaths* in mapping the bed of the English Channel, and Didier Robert de Vaugondy (1726-86), son of the great Robert de Vaugondy. The most monumental French contribution to mapmaking development, however, was made by César-François Cassini (1714-84) and his son, who carried out a complete triangulation and survey of the whole of France and published the results of the survey in the form of the *Carte Géometrique de la France* at a scale of 1:86,400 in 182 sheets. The first sheet of the series pre-dated the Ordnance Survey's first sheet of its one inch to one mile series of Britain by half a century and the series as a whole had far-reaching repercussions, not only for France, but for cartography in general.

## Celestial cartography

The history of mapping the heavens is very much intermixed with that of terrestrial cartography for many of the same cartographers were involved and celestial maps often appeared in atlases along with terrestrial ones. The study of celestial cartography, however, has, perhaps not surprisingly, received less attention from cartographic historians than that of mapping the continents and oceans of our known world. Celestial mapping is a highly specialised subject with fundamental differences in approach; terrestrial mapping derives from exploration and survey by land and sea – a largely tangible approach – whereas mapping of the heavens depended solely on what could be viewed from afar, either with the naked eye or by telescope. In mapping land masses symbols could be developed to represent rivers, mountains, woodland, towns and so on but in the case of the skies cartographers drew upon mythology and religion to illustrate constellations, stars and planets. The first printed maps of the stars were made by the great German artist Albrecht Dürer (1471-1528), but the peak of celestial cartography was reached in 1660 with the publication in Amsterdam by Andreas Cellarius of *Atlas Coelestis seu Harmonia Macrocosmica*, containing twenty-nine beautifully designed, hand-coloured copper engravings. A number of terrestrial atlases included twin-hemisphere celestial maps and the seventeenth century was notable for the production of numerous terrestrial and celestial globes, among which those by Willem Janszoon Blaeu were outstanding. In Britain the Astronomer Royal, John Flamsteed, published his *Atlas Coelestis* (1729) and in Germany Johann Gabriel Doppelmayr (1671-1750), a Nuremberg professor of mathematics as well as a cartographer, prepared an outstanding celestial atlas which was published by Johann Baptist Homann in 1742.

# 4
# Regional mapping in Britain, 1579-1700

Before the late sixteenth century the countries comprising the British Isles had been mapped in various combinations: the whole of the British Isles as seen in various editions of Ptolemy; Britain, i.e. England, Wales and Scotland; England and Wales, exemplified by Humphrey Lhuyd's *Angliae Regni* in Ortelius's *Theatrum*, 1573; Scotland, Wales, England and Ireland as separate entities. In each case the country or countries were mapped as large units. From Elizabethan times, however, until the beginning of the nineteenth century the county became the basic unit for mapwork and it was only the advent of the Ordnance Survey with its accurate one inch to one mile series on national sheet lines that marked the beginning of the end for the county map and the private county surveyor. Nevertheless it was not quite the death knell of private cartography for numerous firms continued to produce atlases and maps in great numbers. Indeed, many such firms remain in existence at the present time.

By 1570 the time was ripe for cartographic development in Britain. In Europe, Flemish mapmakers, using their skills in the art of copper engraving, had wrested cartographic supremacy from Rome and Venice and a number of Flemish Protestant refugees began to introduce these new talents into England. Surveying techniques and instruments were improving rapidly and several treatises on the art of surveying were published. One such was the *Pantometria* (1571) of Leonard Digges in which he describes an instrument of his own invention which resembled a modern theodolite. The Elizabethan age was one of commercial prosperity and also one of intellectual attainment. The arts enjoyed the sponsorship of landed gentry who came into the possession of great estates as a result of the confiscation and redistribution of monastic lands. This reallocation of land led to a demand for new estate maps, a demand which brought about the creation of a new body of professional surveyors known as 'land-meaters'. From the ranks of this body emerged one of the great figures of British cartography – Christopher Saxton.

## Saxton's Atlas of England and Wales (1579)

Saxton, who was born in the hamlet of Dunningley near Wakefield *c*.1542, was commissioned by a Suffolk gentleman,

*A detail from Saxton's Lancashire map in his 'Atlas of England and Wales' (1579) with stippled sea areas and 'sugar loaf' hills roughly graded to suggest relative heights. Courtesy: University of Liverpool (H.49.45).*

Thomas Seckford, to survey and map all the counties of England and Wales. This daunting task was completed in a remarkably short space of time for Saxton's first two maps were engraved in 1574, followed by others in rapid succession. The complete work, consisting of a general map of England and Wales and thirty-four county maps, was published in 1579 as *An Atlas of England and Wales*. To Saxton, and also to Seckford, without whose patronage the work would have been impossible, goes the credit for producing what was the first national atlas to be produced in any country. Yorkshire-born folk can be very proud of Saxton and he, in turn, seems to have been inordinately proud of his birthplace for the name of Dunningley, representing only a cluster of houses, appears, not only on his fine double-page map of Yorkshire but also, more surprisingly, on his general map of England and Wales. A ten-year privilege was granted to Saxton by Queen Elizabeth I to publish and market his maps and he was also awarded his own coat of arms, the sole English mapmaker to receive such an honour. The Queen had shown interest in the project throughout and Saxton included the Tudor royal arms on each map together with those of Thomas Seckford.

41

Very little is known about Saxton himself nor, indeed, about his methods of work but it is clear that he was an original surveyor, travelling the countryside on horseback and making compass sketches or using a plane table to plot his rough maps. To assist him, an open letter was sent by the Queen to local mayors and justices of the peace ordering that Saxton should be conducted to any suitable high place from which he could view the surrounding country and that he should be assisted by the most knowledgeable local people. The benefits of such assistance notwithstanding, there is little doubt that Saxton must have referred to earlier topographical works such as the manuscript itinerary of John Leland and the *Perambulation of Kent* by William Lambarde. Without such reference material it seems highly unlikely that the survey could have been completed so quickly.

It was not easy to find English engravers who were skilled enough in the craft of copper engraving to engrave the draft maps surveyed and drawn up by Saxton. To overcome this problem Seckford turned to Flemish Protestant refugees. Nine maps in the atlas were signed by Remigius Hogenberg, five by Leonard Terwoort – a particularly flamboyant engraver – and two by Cornelis de Hooghe. Through their work for Saxton the skill of the Flemings became fully recognised in England. Three English engravers did work for Saxton: Augustine Ryther, whose signature 'Anglus' distinguished him from the Flemings; Francis Scatter and Nicholas Reynolds. Their work was perhaps more restrained in its ornamentation than that of the Flemings but Ryther's maps in particular are among the finest in the atlas. In general the Saxton maps are among the most decorative of all time, the product of an exuberant age, displaying a wealth of ornamentation to which brilliant colouring was often added after printing. Today the aesthetic appeal of Saxton's maps, allied to their historic importance, has made them eagerly sought by collectors. A complete Saxton atlas, in the unlikely event of one coming up for auction, would command a very high price indeed and even individual maps are very expensive. The price of the latter varies with what the demand is likely to be: for example, a map of a populous county such as Essex is certain to be priced much higher than one with a small population such as Merionethshire. As Saxton's maps are so very scarce it is fortunate that high-quality facsimile reproductions have been produced by the British Museum.

Saxton's engravers used a freer style of lettering than that used on woodcut maps for the graver used in copper engraving could be handled almost as easily as a pen. Nevertheless it should be remembered that the craftsman, when engraving the thick copper sheets, had perforce always to work in reverse so that the printed map made from the copper engraving had all its lettering and detail reading the right way round. The restraint of the fine scripts used on the face of the maps is offset by flamboyant 'swash' lettering used to fill up the sea areas and to indicate the names of adjacent counties.

Saxton made good use of conventional symbols to represent the human and natural features of the landscape but provided no explanation, key or legend. A prominent feature is the depiction of hills, engraved to resemble conical sugar loaves shaded on the eastern slopes and coloured green or brown (though the colouring has no particular significance). There is no attempt at scale in the portrayal of hills though there is evidence of an apparent intent to suggest relative size: for example, Pendle Hill and Ingleborough on the Lancashire map appear taller than the rest. Rivers are clearly and prominently shown by a double line with the important bridging points shown by two parallel lines drawn across the course of the stream. Roads are surprisingly omitted, possibly implying that Saxton intended his work more as a graphic record of the topography and the relative positions of places than as a practical aid to travellers. Woodland is symbolised by groups of delicately engraved trees and if maps by the different engravers are studied it will be seen that each used slightly varying versions of the tree symbol. Great parks are graphically portrayed by a pale fence surrounding a cluster of trees.

Saxton obviously regarded the accurate position of settlements as of paramount importance and used a dot within a circle to show the centre of each place. This circle forms part of a more elaborate symbolisation for villages and towns – villages being located by a church or tower drawn in elevation, towns by a small group of buildings and cities by a sizeable cluster of buildings and churches.

County boundaries are prominently drawn and often emphasised by a band of colour. Hundred boundaries, on the other hand, are shown on only five maps, despite the fact that the hundred remained an important administrative unit at the time.

Sea areas presented a challenge to the engravers' flair for extravagant display and, though the sea itself was shown soberly enough by a stippled or dot pattern, a variety of craft sailed across its surface along with frolicking mermaids, sea monsters and fish. It was often in the spacious sea areas, too, that the engraver placed his ornamental cartouches, heraldry, distance scales, north pointer and similar features.

The words *'Christophorus Saxton descripsit'* appear on each map together with Seckford's motto *'Pestis patriae pigricies'* on the early maps, this wording being altered on later maps to *'Industriam naturam ornat'*. The maps are enclosed in narrow borders resembling moulded picture frames in varied styles. Each map measures 18¼ inches by 15 inches (464 mm by 381 mm) and all were designed to fit the same page size in the atlas. Consequently there are variations in scale from approximately four miles to one inch to two miles to one inch. There are also variations in composition: for instance, Yorkshire, a very large county, occupies a double-page spread while some of the smaller counties are grouped two, three, four or even five to a page. Generally, however, individual counties have a page to themselves.

## *Philip Symonson's map of Kent, 1596*

Although Symonson did not produce a series of county maps, his map of Kent, published in 1596 and engraved by Charles Whitwell, is worthy of special mention as it is arguably the finest example of Elizabethan county mapmaking. It is exceptionally detailed and, like the maps of Symonson's contemporary John Norden, it shows major roads. Towns are symbolised by groups of buildings and villages by a church. These church symbols are a great feature of Symonson's map in that they are immediately recognisable portrayals of the church they represent. Moreover, Symonson introduced a new innovation, that of a circle containing a dot at the church door. Distances were measured between these dots. Windmills are also shown realistically and delightfully while one other important innovation is the distinguishing of the navigable portion of the Medway.

## *John Norden's Speculum Britanniae*

John Norden (1548-1626) was a Somerset man and, like Saxton, was an estate surveyor of considerable ability as well as a cartographical innovator. Unlike Saxton, however, he was beset by financial difficulties and his ambitious scheme for a series of county histories illustrated with maps and entitled *Speculum Britanniae* failed through lack of patronage when only five counties had been completed. Norden, conscious of the deficiencies in other atlases – the lack of roads on Saxton's maps, for example; the need for an English translation of Camden's *Britannia*; the weight and bulk of most atlases – wished to produce a work which would be of greater practical value to the public, providing improved maps along with information about the archaeology, industry, agriculture and history of each county. Only two sections of *Speculum Britanniae* (literally 'A Mirror of Britain'), those dealing with Middlesex (1593) and Hertfordshire (1598) were published during Norden's lifetime. His admirable survey of Cornwall was not published until 1728, Essex not until 1840. Norden also produced some larger county maps, those of Sussex (1595), Surrey

(1594) and Hampshire (c.1595) being printed. His maps introduced several new features. They were the first county maps to delineate roads though Emmison and Skelton[2] state that their examination of four copies of the Essex map reveals so many discrepancies in the mapping of the Essex roads that their portrayal must be treated with caution. The triangular table of distances, by which mileages between places could easily be read off, was introduced into Britain by Norden and is still used effectively today. So, too, is his reference system in which he surrounded his maps with a frame of double lines divided into sections containing figures along the top edge and letters down the side giving a system through which any place can be located quickly by reference to its grid square. Tables of conventional signs were included, listing such items as 'market townes, parrishes, hamletes, noblemens' howses, howses of gent' etc. The quality of Norden's work is evident from the fact that later mapmakers copied his maps, where available, in preference to those of Saxton.

## William Smith's maps of 1602-3 (formerly known as the 'Anonymous Series')

These maps of twelve counties, apparently designed to form part of a single series, for long remained the work of an unknown mapmaker but are now credited to the herald William Smith (1550-1618), who, apart from this series, produced *A Description of England* containing plans and profiles of towns. Smith's handsome county maps are based on Saxton's and Norden's work but incorporate additional place-names, roads, hundred boundaries and names, and a table of conventional signs. They are engraved in the Flemish style with outstandingly good calligraphy and are thought to be the work of Jodocus Hondius. Compared with Saxton and Speed maps, their ornamentation is very restrained.

## William Camden's Britannia, 1607

The 1607 edition of *Britannia* by the antiquary William Camden included a set of county maps which were notable in that, unlike the Saxton atlas, each county was given an individual map. The Camden maps are based on Saxton and Norden and the unwary collector is occasionally misled into thinking they are original Saxtons. This is a trap which can be easily avoided for the two sets are markedly dissimilar. Camden's maps are much smaller, measuring only about 10 inches by 14 inches (250 mm by 350 mm), and were engraved by William Kip and William Hole. They are less detailed and not so decorative as Saxton's maps but, nevertheless, are worth collecting for the clarity of the engraving and their attractive appearance, particularly when hand-coloured.

*Part of the Lancashire map from Speed's 'The Theatre of the Empire of Great Britaine' (1611). More decorative than Saxton's map of the same area, Speed's work is noteworthy for its clarity, ornamentation and fine calligraphy. Courtesy: University of Liverpool (H.17.2).*

### John Speed (1552-1629)

From the early seventeenth century mapmaking in Britain was dominated by London publishers and it was the London firm of John Sudbury and George Humble which launched what has been perhaps the most popular British cartographic venture of all time, John Speed's *The Theatre of the Empire of Great Britaine*, first published in 1611-12.

Speed, born at Farndon in Cheshire, was a tailor's son and followed his father's profession for a time, being admitted to the freedom of the Merchant Taylors' Company in 1580. After his marriage Speed lived in Moorfields and his great enthusiasms were studying antiquity, writing religious works and drawing maps. His antiquarian pursuits found him a patron in the person of Sir

*Inset plan of the city of York from the map of the West Riding of Yorkshire in Speed's 'Theatre' (1611). Courtesy: University of Liverpool (H.17.2).*

Fulke Greville, who provided a stipend so that Speed might devote his time to historical research and mapmaking. Speed's *Theatre* was originally intended to illustrate what was to be the major work, a *History of Great Britaine*, but, interestingly, while the latter is

The map of Lancashire from Pieter van den Keere's 'miniature Speed' atlas of 1627. The cartouche resembles fretwork but the map itself is plain.

now forgotten the maps grow ever more popular. Speed, as he freely admits, was no originator, confessing in an oft quoted remark that 'I have put my sickle into other men's corne'. Unlike Saxton, the practical surveyor travelling around making surveys and accumulating information, Speed was a compiler who worked in library and study assembling his material and preparing rough layouts for the engraver which included all the information to appear on the final printed maps.

Speed's maps are highly decorative, being engraved in Amsterdam by the unrivalled craftsman, artist and scholar Jodocus Hondius, whose skill in blending the material supplied by Speed into a coherent and attractive design entitles him to a sizeable share of the credit for the *Theatre's* success.

Despite the attractiveness of his maps, Speed made no great contribution to cartographic progress. His major innovation was the inclusion of a small inset plan of the county town on each map. These rather delightful little plans were culled from the work of John Norden, William Smith and William Cunningham and were engraved in bird's eye view. They form the first comprehensive collection of English and Welsh town plans and as such were a useful step forward in what was otherwise a somewhat stagnant period in British mapmaking. Portraits of significant historical figures associated with particular counties were also inserted on the maps and occasionally there are engravings of buildings, such as Old St Paul's and Westminster Abbey on the map of Middlesex. Hundred boundaries were a useful feature but Speed failed to include roads. In general the detail resembles that of Saxton with sugar-loaf hills, woodland and parks, and churches or grouped buildings for villages and towns. The hills emphasised by Saxton remain prominent but Speed reduced the number of smaller hills, to little detriment, for the hummocky symbols used by Saxton were no more than an indication of hilly country and not a precise portrayal of individual hills. Speed's maps were reissued and reprinted many times until the mid eighteenth century. They were issued in black and white only, with any colouring applied by hand to order.

## Michael Drayton's Poly-Olbion maps (1612-22)

*Poly-Olbion* was illustrated with a set of eighteen curious little regional maps which were engraved by William Hole. They are of minimal cartographic interest and are quite the oddest set of maps

*One of the curious regional maps which illustrate the eighteen songs by Michael Drayton in 'Poly-Olbion' (1612). Little topographical detail is provided but the maps are covered with symbolic and mythological figures.*

showing counties ever to be produced. Topographical detail is confined to rivers, woods, hills and a few towns. No boundaries appear and each map covers parts of several counties. Allegorical figures, water nymphs, hunters and animals are posed over the landscape and the maps include neither title nor scale of distances.

## Pieter van den Keere: the miniature Speed atlas of 1627

Reduced copies of Saxton's county maps were engraved in 1599 by Pieter van den Keere, or Petrus Kaerius, for a proposed pocket edition of the atlas. This came to naught, however, and the plates came into the hands of Speed's publisher, George Humble, who in 1527 issued forty maps by van den Keere, together with twenty-three new maps copied from Speed, as a pocket atlas for the general public – *England, Wales, Scotland and Ireland described and abridged... from a farr larger volume done by John Speed*. The maps are attractive with plain cartouches but their small dimensions, $4^3/4$ inches by 3 inches (121 mm by 76 mm), mean that some counties look very crowded with place-names. Each map is accompanied by descriptive text from Speed's larger atlas.

## Thomas Jenner

In 1643 Thomas Jenner, a London bookseller, printseller and engraver, issued a *Direction for the English Traviller* consisting of a set of small thumb-nail maps, each with a triangular table of distances. Jenner also published a notable map of England and Wales known as the *Quartermaster's Map* because of its use during the Civil War. This map was engraved by the renowned Wenceslas Hollar on six sheets which folded in such a way that the map would fit handily into a large pocket.

## Joannes Blaeu (1596-1673)

In 1645 Joannes (Joan or John) Blaeu published a set of maps of English and Welsh counties as Part IV of *Theatrum Orbis Terrarum, sive Atlas Novus*. These were derived from Speed but set new standards of elegance in craftsmanship and design. Scotland and Ireland were not included but appeared in 1654 as Part V of *Atlas Novus* and in 1662 as Volume VI of the magnificent *Atlas Maior* or *Grand Atlas*.

While the Blaeu county maps may be regarded as superb examples of engraving and design they add little either to our topographical knowledge or to cartographic development. Blaeu still made no attempt to delineate roads and he dispensed with Speed's inset plans. The detail is generally similar to earlier maps but neater and more delicately engraved. Symbols are smaller and there is a lack of extravagant ornament for its own sake, even sea

*Section of Blaeu's map of Denbigh and Flint (1645).*

areas being sparingly adorned. The calligraphy is especially beautiful and so, too, is the way in which the several elements of each map are blended into a logical, balanced composition.

51

## *Joannes Jansson (1596-1664)*

The rival establishments of Blaeu and Jansson had competed – not entirely amicably, for they were always ready to criticise each other's work – to produce an atlas containing county maps of the British Isles. Blaeu's was completed and published a year ahead of Jansson's. Like his rival, Jansson based his work on that of Speed and if the two sets of maps are compared it will be observed that the Dutch engravers, hardly surprisingly, made several errors in transcribing British place-names. In Cheshire, for instance, the engravers have in over twenty cases wrongly transcribed a letter or arbitrarily abbreviated a name. Jansson tended to be rather more flamboyant than Blaeu, adorning his seas, for example, with elaborate compass roses and sweeping lettering.

A feature of both the Blaeu and Jansson atlases is the splendidly architectural composition of their title pages, similar in conception though different in execution. Each bears an architectural design supporting the royal coat of arms and incorporating figures of Danes, Romans, Normans and Saxons in recesses with the figure of Britannus very prominent. Each design has a cartouche below the imprint and a rectangular title panel. The title pages of these great atlases would make a rewarding study; a later example of an architecturally inspired title-page design is found in Jaillot's *Atlas Nouveau* (1689) and it is revealing to observe how these three great mapmakers interpreted a similar theme.

Both the Blaeu and Jansson atlases appeared in many editions and in several languages, the textual matter being printed on the reverse of the maps.

## *Richard Blome (died 1705)*

Blome, a cartographer and compiler of books on heraldry and topography, issued *Britannia*, containing a set of county maps, in 1673. The maps were of indifferent quality with crude lettering and ornamentation and are generally pirated from earlier works. Nevertheless they have a superficially 'quaint' appearance and are very popular with present-day collectors.

## *Robert Morden (died 1703)*

During the seventeenth century the London map trade was largely concentrated in two areas: firstly in and around Cornhill; and secondly in St Paul's Churchyard and the vicinity of Newgate and Cheapside. Robert Morden, bookseller, publisher and cartographer, worked at the Atlas in Cornhill from 1668 to 1703 and was responsible for engraving county maps for Edmund Gibson's 1695 translation of William Camden's *Britannia*. The preface to this edition states: 'The maps are all newly engrav'd, either

*Eastern section of Robert Morden's map of Bedfordshire in William Camden's 'Britannia' (1695), a plain map which features a triple set of scales of distance bars showing 'great', 'middle' and 'small' miles.*

according to Surveys never publish'd or according to such as have been made and printed since Saxton and Speed. Where actual Surveys could be had, they were purchas'd at any rate; and for the rest, one of the best copies extant was sent to some of the most knowing Gentlemen in each county, with a request to supply the defects, rectify the positions, and correct the false spellings. And that nothing might be wanting to render them as complete and accurate as might be, this whole business was committed to Mr Robert Morden, a person of known abilities in these matters, who took care to revise them, to see the slips of the Engraver mended, and the corrections, return'd out of the several Counties, duly inserted. Upon the whole, we need not scruple to affirm, that they are by much the fairest and most correct of any that have yet appear'd.' Although Morden's maps incorporate some innovations they can hardly be said to live up to this fulsome panegyric. Neither in craftsmanship nor in design do they compare with Blaeu or Jansson. On the credit side Morden undertook considerable revision of place-name spellings and many names appear on his maps in the form used today. The Morden maps include a network of roads and he uses three scales of distance to represent 'great', 'middle' and 'small' miles, which appear to be 2430, 2200 and 1830 yards respectively.

Following a precedent set in a map of Hertfordshire (1676) by John Seller, Morden used London (St Paul's and not, as later, Greenwich) as his prime meridian. His cartographic output was large and included a set of small county maps ($4^3/4$ inches by $5^3/4$ inches; 121 mm by 146 mm) in *The New Description and State of England* (1701) as well as a pack of playing cards bearing tiny county maps (1676). This set has been reproduced in facsimile (1972) by Harry Margary, Lympne Castle, Kent.

# 5
# Regional mapping in Britain, 1700-1860

There was a marked contrast in cartographic development between the two halves of the eighteenth century. Before 1750 there was little originality and not much indication of the striking developments which were to occur later in the century – developments which established mapmaking in Britain on a firm scientific basis. In the early eighteenth century there was continued reworking of earlier material and further reprints of Saxton, Speed and others continued to appear. Such innovations as did occur related not so much to map detail as to secondary matters, the depiction of antiquities in the outer margins of Herman Moll's 1724 set of county maps being one example, the use of copious descriptive notes on the face of Bowen and Kitchin's maps being another.

The second half of the century, however, began highly propitiously with the Royal Society of Arts encouraging prospective surveyors with the award of an annual prize to be awarded for a survey of any county at the large (for those days) scale of one inch to one mile. This award sparked off a profusion of county surveys and thenceforward the one-inch scale was established as the standard scale and remained so until replaced by the 1:50,000 Ordnance Survey series in 1974/6. Apart from the publication of such large-scale county maps, two other significant events occurred in the latter half of the eighteenth century. In 1791 the Ordnance Survey was established (first known as the Trigonometrical Survey), followed by the founding of the Hydrographic Office in 1795, thus putting both map and chart making on an official footing. In spite of this, private county surveys continued until well into the nineteenth century.

## Herman Moll (died 1732)

Moll, a Dutchman who came to London in 1688, was a prolific publisher and engraver of maps and atlases, as well as an inveterate critic of his rivals. On his map of South America other publishers are angrily dismissed as 'ignorant pretenders' and on his world map he says of his fellow countrymen: 'as for ye Dutch maps all of 'em yet extant, are much alike and far enough from Correctness.' Yet Moll had little reason to criticise: for example, his set of county maps in *A New Description of England and Wales* (1724)

*Hermann Moll's rather plain map of Huntingdonshire from 'A New Description of England and Wales' (1724). The main interest of Moll's county maps lies in the marginal illustrations of antiquities.*

displayed little originality and unremarkable craftsmanship. They are, however, distinctive in one respect: in the margins of the maps, engravings of antiquities are displayed. The Lancashire map, for instance, has engravings of Roman relics discovered at Ribchester, Upholland and Standish. Otherwise map detail is derived from earlier sources such as Ogilby, Norden and Speed for there were still no copyright laws to prevent the plagiarism of other publishers' work. It was only in 1734 that the first Copyright Act was introduced in Britain.

### George Bickham and The British Monarchy (1754)

George Bickham (1684-1771) published *The British Monarchy*, a volume of 188 plates of historical notes with forty-three plates of views of English and Welsh counties. They are referred to as views rather than maps for they are merely perspective sketches drawn from a suitable foreground eminence (real or imaginary) with the county stretching away into the distance. Much of each plate is occupied by a foreground scene showing, in Bickham's words, 'a pleasing Landscape...with a variety of Rustic Figures, Ruins &c and the names of the Principal Towns and Villages, intersperced according to their apparent situation'. The topographical detail included is minimal: in the case of Westmorland, for example, only eleven towns, two rivers and 'Winander Meer' appear. The descriptive text of the volume is written in Bickham's elegant calligraphy for he was a celebrated writing master who wrote various books on the subject, including *The Universal Penman*.

### John Rocque (died 1762)

A significant figure who produced some of the finest maps of the eighteenth century was the Huguenot immigrant surveyor John Rocque. Before 1750 Rocque was employed in the preparation of plans of great houses and during this time developed a strikingly effective way of engraving pasture, gardens, heath, cultivated land and other forms of land use. This talent is seen to great effect on his fine county maps of Shropshire, Middlesex, Berkshire and Surrey and especially on his remarkable large-scale plan of the Cities of London and Westminster (1746), a year in which he published another fine plan of London and the country 10 miles (16 km) around. In addition to his unique differentiation between categories of land use, Rocque drew hills in plan with lighting apparently coming from above so that the tops appeared white. Lines were drawn down the slopes, thicker to indicate where the gradient was steeper.

Rocque issued a set of small county maps, each 6 inches by 7³⁄₄ inches (152 mm by 197 mm) in *The English Traveller* (1746), a volume which was reissued in 1753, 1762 and 1764 as *The Small British Atlas*. Rocque had a large output of publications, a contemporary advertisement of his work listing over seventy items, among them outstanding plans of Dublin and Bristol.

## Literary periodicals

Around the middle of the eighteenth century newly established periodicals such as *The London Magazine or Gentleman's Monthly Intelligencer* and *The Universal Magazine of Knowledge and Pleasure* were using maps as illustrations. A set of county maps appeared in the former magazine between 1747 and 1760 while fifty-one maps by Emanuel Bowen, Thomas Kitchin and R. W. Seale were published in *The Universal Magazine* between 1747 and 1766.

## The Large English Atlas of Emanuel Bowen and Thomas Kitchin

Among the most interesting maps of the mid eighteenth century were those prepared by Bowen and Kitchen for *The Large English Atlas* (1760). Bowen, an engraver and printseller, planned an atlas of county maps which were to be the largest and most detailed so far. His scheme eventually bore fruit when *The Large English Atlas* was published but his monetary resources were insufficient

*Eighteenth-century decoration – a vignette of county life from Nottinghamshire in Emanuel Bowen and Thomas Kitchin's 'Large English Atlas' (1760).*

to carry the project through alone and he joined forces with Kitchin, another London engraver and publisher. They shared the engraving of the maps almost equally but Middlesex was the work of R. W. Seale and differs from the rest in that it incorporates the arms of the ninety-two City livery companies and of the City of London. Before the publication of the complete atlas the county maps were issued singly and consequently have differing dates of publication. Cornwall, for example, is dated 1750, Cheshire 1751 and Lancashire 1752. These were the largest county maps to appear up to their time of publication (27 inches by 20 inches; 686 mm by 508 mm) but the scales vary with the size of the county and the way it fits the page. The inclusion of a dedication to the Lord Lieutenant of the county, together with a list of the 'Seats of the nobility &c' indicates the promoters' awareness of the need for attracting local interest and subscriptions to help finance publication.

The most distinctive feature of Bowen and Kitchin maps is the inclusion of copious descriptive notes on the face of the map between boundary and frame. These relate to the history and topography of each county. Each map bears a splendid cartouche or vignetted scene of county life. The titles are invariably 'An Accurate Map of...' and a smaller rococo-style cartouche contains the dedication. The borders are formed by thick outer lines with double inner lines marked off in degrees and minutes, while the maps themselves are covered by a graticule. Considerable topographical detail is included and the 'explanations' list boroughs, market towns with their market days, villages with R or V to indicate rectory or vicarage, charity schools, parks and post stages.

### The Royal English Atlas of Bowen and Kitchin

Bowen and Kitchin, each of whom had a large output of maps and atlases, issued another fine atlas, the *Royal English Atlas,* in 1762. Smaller in format than the *Large English Atlas,* it was designed on similar lines. The county maps were at a reduced scale and had less elaborate cartouches but a great deal of verbal description was inserted wherever space permitted.

In 1767 *Atlas Anglicanus* with reduced versions of the maps in the two larger atlases was published with the imprint 'By the late Emanuel Bowen, Geographer to His Majesty George IId and Thomas Bowen. Printed for T. Kitchin, No. 59, Holborn Hill'.

### County surveys at the one inch to one mile scale

By the mid eighteenth century Bowen had attempted to encompass England and Wales at a reasonably large scale. Individual counties had, moreover, been surveyed at a scale of one inch to one mile and, of these, Henry Beighton's map of Warwickshire,

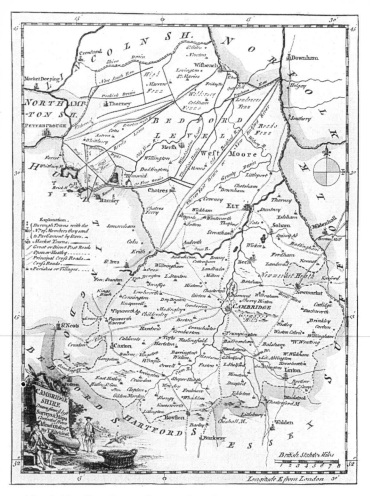

*'Cambridgeshire Drawn from ye best Surveys & Maps Corrected from Astronl Observns, by Thomas Kitchin' (1786).*

surveyed 1722-5, is outstanding, partly because it was one of the first county maps to be soundly based on trigonometrical survey. Beighton, an accomplished surveyor, illustrated the framework of triangles he used in making his survey in the bottom right-hand corner of his map, together with the surveying instruments used, including a 'plotting-table' which he had invented in 1721. A remarkably wide range of features is depicted on the map,

60

reflecting the whole life and economy of the county: parish churches, chapels, depopulated places, seats of nobility, chases, parks, kings' houses, monasteries, castles, Roman ways and stations, battles, garrisons, coal mines, pumping engines, mills and medicinal waters. The inclusion of shields bearing subscribers' names is once again evidence of the practice of financing production by soliciting private subscription.

Beighton's map was well ahead of its time and it was only after 1750 that much progress was made in mapping England at the one-inch scale. By the close of the century, however, the whole country, together with parts of Wales and Scotland, had been mapped at this scale or larger.

## The Royal Society of Arts Award

Scientific mapmaking received its major stimulus from the Society for the Encouragement of Arts, Manufactures and Commerce (known since 1847 as the Royal Society of Arts). The Society's original objective was the raising of public funds with which to provide awards for meritorious discoveries and inventions in art, industry and commerce. In 1755 William Borlase submitted to his friend Henry Baker, one of the most scientifically minded members of the Society, a project for the Society's consideration in these terms: 'I would submit to you as a Friend whether the State of British Geography be not very low, and at present wholly destitute of any public encouragement. Our maps of England and its counties are extremely defective... if among your premiums for Drawings some reward were offered for the best Plan, Measurement and actual Survey of City or District, it might move the Attention of the Public towards Geography, and in time, perhaps, incline the Administration to take this matter into their hands... and employ proper persons every year, from actual Surveys to make accurate Maps of Districts, till the whole island is regularly surveyed.' This was a plea, therefore, not only for a national survey but also, with foresight, for regular revision of maps. For various reasons it was not acted upon until 1759, when the Society published an advertisement offering an award of not more than £100 for an original survey at a scale of one inch to one mile.

Between 1759 and 1801 twenty-three surveyors submitted claims and thirteen county maps were successful, the first being Benjamin Donn's map of Devonshire. Two important points were made by Donn in the proposals for his map: first, 'As the Accuracy, and consequently the Value, of a map must chiefly depend on the Correctness of the Position and horizontal Distances of the Principal Places, particular care will be taken to determine these in a new and rational Method, by the Assistance of a curious set of Instruments, Trigonometrical Calculations, and Astronomical Observation'; and second, 'The Roads, (at least the High Roads) will be actually measured'. Donn's map, therefore, was established on firm scientific foundations and the actual survey took five and a half years in which over 6000 miles (9600 km) of roads and rivers were surveyed, together with the angles of towers and hills.

Notwithstanding the scientific construction of the new maps, the decorative arts were not entirely forgotten. Many maps were embellished with large splendid cartouches. Essex, for example, published in 1777 by John Chapman and Peter André – one of the most detailed county maps – features a cartouche depicting a fulling mill with cloth beaters. Andrews and Dury's Wiltshire (1773) includes a scene symbolising the products of the county with sheep, wheat, milking and a bale of cloth. This vignette was designed by G. B. Cipriani and engraved by T. Caldwell, the practice of engaging special craftsmen for a cartouche being fairly common at the time.

An outstanding figure in mid eighteeenth-century cartography was Thomas Jefferys, Geographer to George III and an authority on North America. Besides engraving Donn's prize-winning map of Devon, Jefferys himself was responsible for publishing maps of Bedford, Huntingdon, Buckingham, Cumberland, Oxford, Durham, Westmorland and a specially fine twenty-sheet map of Yorkshire. He depicted relief by *hachuring* (finely engraved lines drawn down the slopes, thick where the slope was steep and thinner where it was more gradual). This technique brought out prominent hills and deep valleys clearly but was less successful in presenting an overall picture of the topography.

Several of the new large-scale maps included inset plans of principal towns or views of prominent buildings. Isaac Taylor's Gloucestershire (1777) includes engravings of castles; Chapman and André's Essex features a plan of Colchester; Jefferys's Buckinghamshire has an inset plan of Buckingham.

Various surveyors were at work throughout England, some producing maps of several counties. Andrew Armstrong published maps of Northumberland (a winner of the Royal Society award), Durham, Lincoln and Rutland; William Yates, a Liverpool customs officer, surveyed Lancashire, Staffordshire and Warwickshire; Peter Burdett, a Derbyshire artist, made maps of Cheshire and Derbyshire; others such as Joseph Lindley, J. Prior, W. Day, T. Milne, J. Hodskinson, J. Evans and T. Eyre mapped individual counties. In some cases the surveyors provided evidence of the scientific basis of their maps by including triangulation diagrams. The triangulation system used in county maps of the Midlands and north-western England can be said to anticipate the principal triangulation of the Ordnance Survey and the fact that the same stations have been selected, in many cases by both private and official surveys, is a pointer to the sound concepts on which the private surveys were founded.

Maps were still issued in black and white only, with hand colouring sometimes added to order. Publication was generally in the form of single sheets and the catalogue of W. Faden, who took over Jefferys's business in Charing Cross and bought up many copper plates of eighteenth-century surveys, gives some idea of map prices in the early nineteenth century: Yates's Lancashire cost £1 12s, Isaac Taylor's four-sheet map of Hereford 16s, Rocque's eighteen-sheet map of Berkshire £1 12s. The average size of an edition of a county map of this kind would be about three hundred copies, of which many would go to subscribers[3]. An extra charge of five shillings would be made for hand colouring and a specially bound edition with title page and printed index such as might be found in the libraries of county gentry would cost a further two guineas.

## John Cary (c.1754-1835)

Despite the domination of this period by large-scale individual county mapmaking, some publishers, of whom John Cary and Charles Smith stood out, were producing small, reasonably priced atlases which were a marked improvement on any similar publications so far.

The cartographic historian Sir H. G. Fordham regarded Cary as the 'most representative, able and prolific of English cartographers' – high praise from one who had made a special study of Cary's life and work. Whether we agree or not with this assessment, it cannot be denied that Cary was a fine craftsman who had a formidable publication list. His *New and Correct English Atlas* (1787) was a quarto volume of forty-six county maps, each accompanied by descriptive text, which were an advance on any comparable set of maps to date for Cary was able to draw freely on the work of larger-scale county surveyors. For Gough's translation of Camden's *Britannia* (1789) Cary engraved fine county maps 16 1/4 inches by 18 1/4 inches (413 mm by 464 mm), which were characterised by clear engraving and a considerable amount of detail including hundred boundaries. The *Traveller's Companion* (1789) was an octavo volume with forty maps of English counties, a general map of England and Wales, and maps of North and South Wales, all printed on one side only of thin paper. At the top of each map is a title panel with the county name lettered against a hatched background. On the left of the panel are the words 'By J. Cary' and on the right 'Engraver'. The imprint 'London. Published Sepr. 1, 1789 by J. Cary, Engraver, No. 188 Strand' appears below the map. Despite their small dimensions, only $3^1/2$ inches by $4^3/4$ inches (89 mm by 121 mm), these maps are clear and legible. Turnpike roads traversed by mail coaches are picked out in blue, other turnpikes in red; a bold type is used to emphasise the names of market towns and distances between places are indicated along the roads. The *Traveller's Companion* was deservedly popular and was reprinted several times up to 1828.

Cary's finest map series appeared in his *New English Atlas* (1809). The title of each map begins 'A New Map of...' and ends 'By John Cary Engraver'. All have the imprint 'London: Published by J. Cary, Engraver & Mapseller No. 181 Strand' together with the date. These were Cary's largest county maps, measuring $18^1/4$ inches by $20^1/4$ inches (464 mm by 514 mm). The atlas, one of the finest products of nineteenth-century mapmaking, was beautifully engraved and, though functional, the maps are attractive, particularly when hand-coloured. The *New English Atlas* was issued in parts between 1801 and 1809, which means that individual counties have varying dates of publication: many are dated 'Sepr. 28, 1801' while others vary from 21st December 1801 to 1st June 1809.

Roads figured prominently on Cary's maps for he was employed by the Postmaster-General to organise the survey of turnpike roads in Great Britain, a task involving 9000 miles (14,000 km) of survey. Decoration is eschewed on all Cary series and this assists his intent to present geographical information clearly and without distraction.

### Charles Smith

Cary's competitor, Charles Smith, published a *New English Atlas* in 1804, well before Cary's work of the same title. The two sets of maps are so similar in style and conception that there has been some inevitable speculation as to whether one or the other had copied his rival's work. An alternative explanation could be that both worked from common sources and it was hardly surprising that they produced maps which were at least factually similar.

The visual similarity, however, is not so easily accounted for. It seems unlikely that a man of Cary's calibre, who had already published a fine atlas in 1787, would stoop to plagiarism of this sort. Nevertheless, each man produced work of exceptional merit which is by no means disgraced when compared with the early one inch to one mile sheets of the Ordnance Survey which were appearing slowly from 1801 onwards.

### Private one-inch scale county mapmaking

The development of the official mapmaking body, the Ordnance

Survey, did not as yet signal the demise of the private county surveyor. Surveyors such as Christopher Greenwood, for example, had their own projects for one-inch scale coverage of the whole nation and, indeed, they were assisted to some extent by the Trigonometrical Survey of the Board of Ordnance, as it was then called, for one of this body's major functions in its early days was to provide private mapmakers with the locations of trigonometrical points.

### Christopher Greenwood (born 1786)

A Yorkshireman, Christopher Greenwood, and the firm of which he was head played a prominent role in early nineteenth-century mapmaking in England. Although his scheme for a national set of one inch to one mile maps did not come to fruition in full, he almost succeeded. After an initial survey of his native county in 1817-18 Greenwood published maps of thirty-four other counties, leaving only six English counties and three in Wales still to be surveyed. His method of promotion was to insert a prospectus in the local press outlining the objectives and methodology of his proposed scheme and to follow this up with a more detailed prospectus which he sent to advance subscribers. An important part of his sales technique was to publish a list of subscribers, headed by nobility but including customers from the business and professional classes. Vignettes of buildings and landscape scenes appeared on several maps and, in his prospectus, Greenwood wrote: 'with a view to render the County Maps as ornamental as useful, the Proprietors will use every means to join superior elegance with minutest accuracy. Vignettes from the pencils of distinguished artists will be added to the Maps of such Counties as furnish appropriate subjects.' Richard Creighton's meticulous engraving of Durham Cathedral on the map of County Durham is an outstanding example of these vignettes.

The map of Worcestershire [4] is typical of the Greenwood series – a large map in four sheets engraved by Neele & Son. The eye is drawn to the flamboyant title and dedication, which are a curious amalgam of typographic styles. This title, *Map of the County of Worcester from Actual Survey made in the Years 1820 & 1821 by C. & J. Greenwood, London. Published by the Proprietors G. Pringle Junr & C. Greenwood, 70 Queen Street, Cheapside, 1st June 1822. Engraved by Neele & Son, 352 Strand,* uses no less than ten different kinds of alphabet and this is quite characteristic of Greenwood maps. The border is formed of a thick line between two fine ones, with a double inner line marked off into degrees and minutes of latitude and longitude. Between the two sets of lines is a wavy hatching with double lines at the outer edge resembling piano keys. This type of border is typical of the time and may have been derived from early Ordnance Survey maps. The maps show considerable human and topographic detail with relief shown, not very satisfactorily, by fine hachuring.

The firm was known as C. & J. Greenwood, Christopher having his younger brother, John, as partner along with G. Pringle and G. Pringle Junior. After 1828, when the business was failing, Greenwood devised two schemes to help bolster the finances. The first was for an atlas of county maps at a scale of approximately three miles to one inch. This was issued in four parts with excellent maps, similar in design to the larger-scale series and engraved by well-known craftsmen. Greenwood himself was not an engraver and the cost of engraving must have been a heavy drain on the company's resources. Greenwood's second and final scheme, which failed to materialise, was for the establishment of a body which would undertake regular revision of the county maps in the Greenwood atlas – an idea reminiscent of that put to the Royal Society of Arts by William Borlase many years earlier. On the final collapse of the Greenwood firm some copper plates were purchased by other publishers, among them Henry Teesdale, whose company itself published a notable county atlas, the *New British Atlas* (1829).

## Andrew Bryant

Another surveyor with ideas of mapping the whole of Britain was Andrew Bryant, whose maps were generally more detailed than Greenwood's and at a larger scale – $1^1/2$ inches to one mile. Bryant succeeded in mapping only thirteen counties but in some cases there was keen rivalry – both men published maps of Surrey in 1823 and Gloucestershire in 1824 – and at times it appears that Greenwood, Bryant and the Ordnance Survey must have been working simultaneously in the same county. Both Greenwood's and Bryant's maps were available in various formats – flat, mounted on common roller, mounted on spring roller folded in case, in case half-bound, coloured or uncoloured – and at prices varying with the luxury of the presentation. The standard subscription for Greenwood's projected series of one-inch maps was 125 guineas or 3 guineas per map.

## Small-scale nineteenth-century atlases

The one-inch scale did not entirely monopolise the nineteenth century and county atlases of varying size and quality continued to be published, along with road books and directories. *Wallis's New Pocket Edition of the English Counties or Traveller's Companion* (1810), which contained forty-four county maps, each 4 inches by

*Thomas Moule's Lancashire map from 'The English Counties Delineated' (1837). Moule's maps represent a brief return to the use of decorative features as a significant part of map design.*

5¹/₂ inches (102 mm by 140 mm), with descriptive text, was typical of the period. In 1829, however, Pigot & Company's *British Atlas* was significant in that its title tells us of the important fact that 'the whole was engraved on steel plates'. The advantage of steel for engraving, compared with copper, was its greater durability, which allowed much longer printing runs.

In 1836 Thomas Moule, a scholar with antiquarian interests, published a set of county maps in *The English Counties Delineated* which are immensely popular with present-day collectors because of their return to the tradition of decorative cartography. The maps, which are small but clearly engraved on steel, have decorative borders, heraldic shields, title cartouches and attractive vignettes of county scenes. They are easily obtainable, reasonably priced and look well when hand-coloured. Modern facsimiles of Moule's maps abound.

J. & C. Walker, who engraved many plates for Greenwood, published their *British Atlas* in 1837 with detailed county maps which later formed the basis for a nineteenth-century cartographic curiosity, *Hobson's Fox-Hunting Atlas* (1850), in which the areas and meeting places of the hunts were superimposed on the original Walker maps.

Many nineteenth-century county atlases can be easily found today and are sold at much lower prices than earlier and scarcer material. They can, moreover, be of particular interest to local historians for their identification of roads, canals, railways etc. A cautionary word is necessary, however, about always taking such information at face value. Some of the maps are notoriously unreliable and, whenever possible, it is wise to check their information against alternative sources.

# 6
## *The formative years of the Ordnance Survey*

Although the official beginnings of the Ordnance Survey date from 1791 the impetus which pushed forward its foundation can be traced to the last Jacobite rising, when Prince Charles Edward, the Young Pretender, at the head of his Highland army, marched as far south as Derby. Lacking support in England, he retreated over the border, to be defeated by the Duke of Cumberland's troops at Culloden in 1746. The subsequent pacification carried out by the Duke of Cumberland in the Highlands was hindered by the lack of good maps. The Deputy Quarter-Master General, Lieutenant-General Watson, determined to make good maps of the Highlands and Colonel Sir Charles Close suggests[5] that it is from the commencement of this mapping of the Highlands, in 1747, that we should perhaps date the first idea of an Ordnance Survey, for the work was carried out, under government orders, by the Army. A dual programme of mapping the Highlands and opening them up with military roads was instituted. The roads were to be constructed under General Wade's supervision and, when complete, would permit rapid troop movements in the event of further Jacobite excursions. The task of mapping began in 1747, and the man chiefly responsible for it was William Roy. The survey was carried out by compass traverses, detail being filled in by field sketching. These historic maps are now stored in the British Museum. In 1765 Roy was made Surveyor-General of Coasts and Engineer for Making and Directing Military Surveys under the Honourable Board of Ordnance, thus establishing a firm connection between the Board of Ordnance and mapmaking.

The pursuance of the War of American Independence hindered progress towards a national survey but in 1783 a new initiative came from the French astronomer M. Cassini de Thury, who argued the scientific advantages of linking the observatories of Paris and Greenwich by precisely surveyed triangulation. His suggestion was adopted in Britain and Roy was placed in charge of operations, his major task being to measure a baseline on Hounslow Heath from which a triangulation system would reach out, linking Greenwich with Dover and subsequently dovetailing with the French triangulation. The baseline measurement was completed in 1784 and, after Roy's death in 1790, triangulation was continued by the Duke of Richmond, Master of the Ordnance.

In 1791 Richmond brought surveying further under the wing of the Ordnance by establishing the Trigonometrical Survey with headquarters alongside those of the Ordnance in the Tower of London. The aims of this new body were to establish an accurate trigonometrical framework for the whole of Britain and to produce a series of one inch to one mile maps – on national sheet lines and not on a county basis. The first map, a four-sheet map of Kent, appeared in 1801 and the next four were of Essex. Like their successors for some time to come, the maps were engraved on copper, allowing thin lines to be clearly printed, as may be well seen if the hachuring on these maps is studied. Alterations to the plates were easy, for the part to be amended had only to be scraped, ground and burnished before re-engraving. These early copper plates measured 36 inches by 24 inches (914 mm by 610 mm) and weighed approximately 35 pounds (16 kg). Before engraving, a draughtsman would prepare a drawing on fine card for the engraver, reducing the larger-scale survey work to the one inch to one mile scale (the survey was mainly at two inches to one mile but in some areas at three inches or six inches to one mile). Roads and lettering would be correctly drawn in and hachuring added with broad strokes. The completed drawing had then to be transferred in reverse to the copper plate. Progress was slow, a single sheet taking months to prepare, but the result was a clear comprehensive study from which the engraver could work at the reduced scale.

The Ordnance maps were an improvement over many late eighteenth-century county maps but there was, nevertheless, some criticism after 1820 as to their accuracy. This may be partly explained by the stringency of the Survey's budget – from 1791 to 1811 a mere £52,000. This may have influenced the surveyors in their attitude to the relative importance of the trigonometrical and topographical stages of the survey for their overriding interest lay with the trigonometrical construction rather than the detailed topographical infilling.

Major-General William Mudge directed the early stages of the survey and was succeeded in 1820 by Captain Colby, under whose directorship the one-inch map took on a lighter and more delicate look, with the finest of hachuring and small neat lettering. By 1840 only Scotland and the six northern counties of England remained unmapped at the one-inch scale. England and Wales south of the Hull-Preston line were covered by sheets 1 to 90 of the *Old Series*. North of this line the sheets of the *Old Series* were reduced from larger-scale (six inches to one mile) surveys but were issued with numbers following on from those of southern England, i.e. 91 to 110. Each sheet number was divided into quarters as the maps were

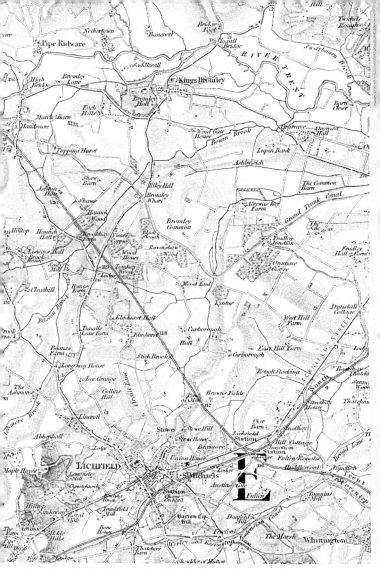

*A section (reduced in scale) of the Ordnance Survey Old Series Sheet 62. 'Published at the Tower of London, Jan. 9th, 1834 by Lieut Colonel Colby of the Royal Engineers. Engraved at the Ordnance Map Office in the Tower under the Direction of Lieut Colonel Colby by Benjn Baker & Assistants. The Writing by Eben Bourne.'*

issued as quarter sheets, thus giving, for example, 91NW, 91SW, 91NE and 91SE. This numbering system was superseded in 1872, when it was decided to carry the six-inch survey southwards. The original quarter sheets were gradually withdrawn and re-numbered to form sheets 1 to 73 of the *New Series*. However, in this volume we are not concerned with Ordnance Survey development beyond the completion of the *Old Series*, sometimes loosely termed the *First Edition*. This had taken seventy years to complete but by 1870 Britain had a scientific triangulation system and a series of maps rivalling anything to be found elsewhere.

No table of conventional signs was issued with the *Old Series* sheets though many symbols are employed. Turnpike and secondary roads are clearly shown with an indication of whether they were fenced or unfenced; tracks are delineated by a double dotted line but footpaths are shown only intermittently. Buildings in villages are solid black but in towns buildings are tinted or hatched. Windmills are delightfully drawn but, unlike some of the county surveys, there is no symbol for watermills, a rather surprising omission in view of their importance. Gardens are shown on the southern sheets but not on the later northern sheets. Occasionally public houses are named, such as the Old Lamb at Kingston Bagpuize, and on certain sheets hotels of especial interest to travellers are named – the Victoria at Llanberis, for example. Unlike our more impersonal modern maps, it was customary to credit the craftsmen involved in the making of the map. We therefore find Ebenezer Bourne constantly credited with the engraving of lettering while Benjamin Baker and his assistants are noted as having engraved the hills. The maps are surrounded by a 'piano-key' type of frame with the scale and imprint usually placed below.

Though lacking consistency and with no absolute uniformity of style, the *Old Series* is a formidable achievement, the first in a succession of Ordnance Survey series of the one inch to one mile map which culminated in the splendid *Seventh Series*, which has now been superseded by the metric 1:50,000 series.

# 7
# Town plans and views

The problem of presenting graphically on a flat sheet of paper the complex layout of a town with its street network, open spaces and varied buildings, all at different levels, is one which has taxed the ingenuity of mapmakers for centuries. Most modern plans present the urban scene to scale as viewed from directly overhead, thus providing an accurate portrayal of the general layout but giving the viewer little impression of the town's visual appearance or the many variations in level. How then have mapmakers attempted to deal with what would appear to be an insoluble problem? Three major techniques have been tried: firstly, the town prospect or view presenting the town as seen in elevation; secondly, to raise the viewpoint by varying degrees so that a bird's eye perspective view is produced – while this could be effective, there were considerable problems of accuracy due to the difficulties of dealing with perspective and scale; thirdly, the viewpoint was raised again so that the urban scene was pictured from directly overhead – the plan view.

Towns had long featured prominently on topographical maps owing to their administrative, political and commercial importance but the town plan as a separate entity only became an important part of British mapmaking in Elizabethan times. Elsewhere we can turn to the books of islands or *Isolario* which gave mariners detailed information about the ports of the Mediterranean region and included plans of harbours and views of towns to supplement the nautical data. Splendid examples are the *Isolario* of Bordone and the *Liber Insularem Archipelagi* (1420) of Cristoforo Buondelmonte, which includes a particularly striking bird's eye view of Constantinople showing very clearly the layout of the city within its wall.

## Woodcut plans

During the late fifteenth century many printed books included woodcut illustrations – portraits, maps, town views – with southern Germany the centre of production. In 1482 Bernhard von Breydenbach made a pilgrimage to the Holy Land and the account of his travels, *Peregrinatio in Terram Sanctam* (Mainz, 1486), contains woodcut views of Venice and other places encountered en route by von Breydenbach and his splendid map of the Holy Land features a dramatic view of Jerusalem.

## Mantua

*A woodcut perspective view of Mantua from Hartmann Schedel's 'Liber Chronicarum' or 'Nuremberg Chronicle' (1493). Courtesy: University of Liverpool.*

The Nuremberg physician Hartmann Schedel included a profusion of woodcut maps, town views and portraits in his encyclopedic *Liber Chronicarum* or *Nuremberg Chronicle* (1493). 645 illustrations were included in all, some of them rather baffling to the reader for in the economical, though misleading, fashion of the day the same portraits appeared in different parts of the book to represent different persons while town views were also repeated at intervals – sixty-nine towns were represented by only twenty-two views. Other sixteenth-century German cosmographiae, particularly Sebastian Münster's *Cosmographia* (1544), were copiously illustrated with woodcut maps, views and portraits.

Not surprisingly, Venice has been favoured with a succession of varied and splendid town plans and views. Of these the finest is

*Pianta Prospettica della Citta* (1500) by J. de' Barbari, who presents Venice as it might be seen from a considerable height above S. Giorgio Maggiore. The incomparable city is spread out before us in great detail and Barbari's large plan, approximately 53 inches by 112 inches (1346 mm by 2845 mm), clearly demonstrates how much can be learned about the constituent features of a city from an accurately drawn pictorial representation of this kind.

In 1552 Hans Lautensack prepared a powerful woodcut prospect of the city of Nuremberg, a work which shows to the full the artistry which can be brought to such a view by an outstanding craftsman. Lautensack provides detailed illustrations of ecclesiastical and domestic architecture and in the foreground, outside the town limits, includes a vigorous scene of harvesting while a group of gentlemen point out and discuss the features of the city skyline.

*Delle Navigationi e Viaggi* (1556), a collection of travellers' tales by the Venetian Giambattista Ramusio, includes delightful woodcut maps and town plans which furnish important documentary information about such fabled cities as the Inca capital, Cuzco; Hochelaga, the ancient Indian city once situated where Montreal now stands; and the Aztec capital of Tenochtitlan.

*Woodcut view of Koblenz at the confluence of the Rhine and Mosel showing the town overshadowed by the imposing fortress of Ehrenbreitstein on the right bank of the Rhine. From Schedel's 'Nuremberg Chronicle' (1493). Courtesy: University of Liverpool.*

## *Engraved plans*

The German geographer Georg Braun, working in conjunction with the famed engraver Frans Hogenberg, published a six-volume set of town plans and views entitled *Civitates Orbis Terrarum* (Cologne, 1572-1618), finely engraved on copper and using all the techniques of urban portrayal known at the time. The towns themselves are often placed in the middle distance and fronted by a colourful scene of local life with figures in appropriate costume. Particularly when hand-coloured, the plates are extraordinarily interesting and attractive, as well as providing documentary evidence of the general appearance of many medieval towns, including several in England and Scotland. Braun and Hogenberg's plan of London entitled *Londinum Feracissimi Angliae Regni Metropolis* and a rather crude woodcut plan attributed to Ralph Agas are the most important surviving early plans of the city. There are striking similarities in the detail of the two plans and it has been suggested that each was based on an early map of the period 1553-9 [6]
.

## *Other pre-Fire plans and views of London*

Among other cartographers who prepared plans and views of London before 1666 are: John Norden, who published small, but detailed plans of London and Westminster (1593); Sebastian Münster (1598); Cornelis Dankerts (*c*.1633); and Thomas Porter (*c*.1655).

## *Post-Fire plans of London*

The Great Fire of 1666 left the city authorities with the problem of rebuilding the city and with the settlement of disputes in respect of property boundaries. New surveys and plans were an immediate necessity and, to this end, John Ogilby and William Morgan were appointed to prepare up-to-date plans. Together they completed the survey in 1676. Ogilby died in the same year and the plan was published by Morgan a year later. It is a remarkable plan, the first accurate plan of the city, in twenty sheets at a scale of approximately 5 inches to 500 feet. In 1682 Morgan published a further plan of the city which also covered the built-up area outside the city boundary. This plan, in twelve sheets, at a scale of 5 inches to 1500 feet, included considerable ornamentation: the title was inscribed on a ribbon with swags and putti; the border incorporates winged heads and a floral design; many views of important buildings and scenes are included, as are lists of officers of state, nobility, City companies, bishops and so on.

## *Matthäus Merian*

Matthaüs Merian, born in Basle in 1592 and a prolific producer of European town plans and views during the seventeenth century, was one of the colossi of historic urban mapmaking. From his Frankfurt workshop, where he employed over twenty craftsmen, Merian published topographies, books of antiquities and books of maps and plans. His twenty-one volume *Theatrum Europaeum* included many engravings of towns and cities in which, like his contemporaries, he used the available techniques of elevation, perspective view and plan. Merian had an inspired gift for lively portrayals of his subject and the town views in particular contain valuable illustrations of the daily life, trade, customs and culture of each place.

## Joan Blaeu

The great seventeenth-century Amsterdam cartographer Joan Blaeu is rightly renowned for the quality and elegance of his atlases, sheet maps, wall maps and globes. His magnificent volumes of urban plans are possibly less familiar though no one opening one of his volumes of Italian towns or his two-volume work devoted to Dutch towns could fail to be entranced by the craftsmanship, the detail, the liveliness, the ornamentation and the detailed portrayal of great churches, important buildings, houses and gardens. Blaeu used a numbering system in conjunction with a reference table to enable individual buildings to be quickly located and by including a linear scale of paces shows a welcome attempt at accuracy.

## Turgot's plan of Paris

Paris, like London and Venice, has been well served by mapmakers: Braun and Hogenberg (1572), Merian (1615) and the Dutchman Claes Jansz Visscher (1618) all provided portrayals of the city which are superb examples of urban cartography, but even these were eclipsed by a twenty-sheet plan drawn in perspective and engraved by Louis Brétez and Claude Lucas to a commission by Michel Etienne Turgot. Dated 1734-9, the plan shows the perspective technique to perfection, presenting the city in great architectural detail, with a lively indication of its day-to-day life. While lacking some of the accuracy of a modern large-scale plan, Turgot provides us with invaluable documentary evidence about the character and layout of mid eighteenth-century Paris.

## Late eighteenth-century plans of London

In 1746 the first thorough survey of London for over fifty years was published by John Tinney, the survey being undertaken by the Huguenot John Rocque, who also published fine plans of Bristol (1742), Exeter (1744) and Shrewsbury (1746) in addition to *A*

*Section of a plan of the Italian city of Aquila from 'Novum Italiae Theatrum', the 1724 edition of Blaeu's magnificent town books of Italy, published by Pierre Mortier in Amsterdam. Courtesy: University of Liverpool.*

*Collection of Plans of the Principal Cities of Great Britain and Ireland* (1764). Rocque's twenty-four sheet plan of London was drawn at a scale of twenty-six inches to one mile, a large scale which enabled him to show an enormous amount of detail with great clarity. It was superbly engraved by John Pine with an elegant border and grand cartouches enclosing the title and the linear scales of distance. A particularly graphic feature is the use of evocative textures and symbolisation to illustrate different types of land use.

Although Rocque's plan is aesthetically pleasing as well as functional, it is perhaps overshadowed in accuracy by Richard Horwood's remarkable thirty-two sheet plan of 1792-9 in which the twenty-six inches to one mile scale (the same as Rocque's) enabled him to locate every house, court and alley. Horwood's original intention was to include the street number of every house and, though he failed to accomplish this task in its entirety, a great many numbers are provided. William Faden issued a second edition of Horwood's plan in 1807, adding eight extra sheets which enabled the burgeoning dock system in the east to be shown. Faden published further editions in 1813 and 1819, thus making available a series of plans which illustrate changes in the city at a time of rapid growth. Horwood's plan, in which 'he took every angle, measured almost every line and after that plotted and compared the whole work', remained the supreme cartographic presentation of London until the Ordnance Survey issued its twenty-five inches to one mile series in the 1860s. Horwood also published, in 1803, a fine six-sheet plan of the rapidly developing port of Liverpool, where he died in poverty in the same year.

Other British towns and cities were not neglected by surveyors in the latter half of the eighteenth century and first half of the nineteenth. Rocque's work has already been mentioned. Others included William Bradford's plan of Birmingham (1754); Isaac Taylor's Hereford (1757); John Eyes's Liverpool (1765); George Perry's Liverpool (1769); William Green's outstanding plan of Manchester and Salford (1794); William Shakeshaft's Preston (1809); and Jonathan Bennison's superb plan of Liverpool (1835).

## Panoramas and prospects

Acting as a complement to the large-scale plans in the mid eighteenth century were the vivid town prospects, eighty-three in all, of places in England and Wales by Samuel and Nathaniel Buck. Published in 1728, when used in conjunction with a large-scale ground plan of the same period the Buck views have much to tell us about the contemporary urban scene. The Buck panorama of London, for example, a five-sheet work, can be allied to Rocque's

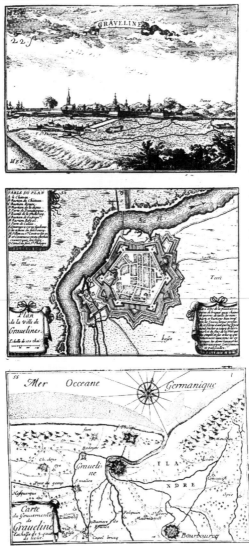

*View, plan and location map of Gravelines from 'Les Plans et Profils des Principal Villes…du Comte de Haynaut' (Paris, c.1760) by Sr. de Beaurain.*

1746 plan to give a telling survey of the layout, life and architecture of the city.

Panoramas and prospects were a feature of newspapers and illustrated magazines of the 1840s, the *Illustrated London News* issuing several and the *Pictorial Times* producing a 'Grand Panorama of the Thames' which was no less than 14 feet (4.27 metres) in length. The popularity of ballooning led to a further increase in the production of perspective plans for the basket of a tethered balloon made an ideal platform from which to record the townscape far below. One splendid example was published by Banks &

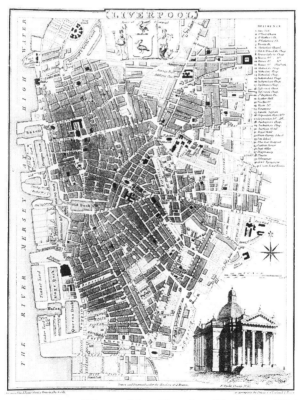

*An attractive plan of Liverpool from 'Beauties of England and Wales' by G. Cole and J. Roper (1804-10).*

Company and portrayed London in great detail as seen from above Hampstead to the north of the city. The technique was a precursor of modern aerial photography using aircraft and spacecraft.

The bird's eye view technique remained popular in the mid nineteenth century with fine examples by George Washington Wilson, who published a view of Aberdeen in 1850 for which he made sketches of buildings and street views at ground level and from tall buildings, and by Nathaniel Whittock, whose output included views of Oxford (1834), Melbourne (1854), Hull (1855) and London (1845, 1849 and 1859). Whittock's outstanding work, however, was an extraordinarily accurate and informative view of York (1858) in which it seems likely that he either sketched or took photographs of the city from a captive balloon.

Numerous directories, gazetteers, guidebooks and local histories were published during the nineteenth century and such works often included maps and town plans. *Plans of the Cities and Boroughs of England and Wales* (1832), an investigation into local government, contained plans by Lieutenant R. K. Dawson RE, which delineated the boundaries of the old boroughs, of proposed boroughs and of parishes established through the Boundaries Act of 1832.

*View of the Representative History of England* (1840) by S. Lewis & Company covered changes due to the Reform Act of 1832 and contained county maps and town plans. The former showed electoral divisions and the latter delineated the 'former and present boundaries of the cities and boroughs'.

Plans were also produced to illustrate property transactions, to delineate the line of a tramway or railway, to illustrate projected development schemes and to accompany the written apportionments of the Tithe Commission under the Tithe Act of 1826. In sum, private mapmakers have left a rich quarry of evidence about the makeup of British towns and cities up to the advent of the national map series of the Ordnance Survey at 1:2500 (twenty-five inches to one mile), which, along with the even larger-scale plans at 1:1056 (five feet to one mile), 1:528 (ten feet to one mile) and 1:500 (10.56 feet to one mile), are a standard reference and working tool of urban historians and local authorities at the present time.

# 8
# Road maps and roadbooks

A major aim of maps throughout their development has been to indicate routes from one place to another. Whenever there has been a new development in means of travel – by sea, road, canal, rail or air – there has been a considerable output of new maps to meet the requirements of those travellers who will use the new routes. This chapter is concerned with the early development of what is probably the most widely used type of specialist map – the road map.

## Roman mapmaking

The Romans, when occupied with the administrative and military needs of their widespread empire, concentrated on surveys designed to aid their administrators and also to facilitate the movements of commercial and military traffic. The earliest extant road map is thought to be a map drawn on the parchment covering of a shield dated AD *c*.200-250 which shows a Roman road leading from Byzantium to the mouth of the Danube[7]. Although it is known that numerous maps were made in Rome, unfortunately there are few survivors. One such map, known only through literary references, was made for the Emperor Augustus by Vipsanius Agrippa and, though no copies survive, it is believed that the most important extant example of a Roman map, the so-called *Tabula Peutingeriana* or *Peutinger Table,* was based on Agrippa's map. The cartographic historian Leo Bagrow writes[8] that around AD 250 a copy was made of an original route map from the first century AD; about AD 350 various improvements were made to this map, mainly relating to the depiction of coastlines and the addition of more islands; about 500 more improvements were made and in the eighth and ninth centuries there were additional amendments. Unfortunately the original map with its extensive series of revisions was lost but a copy which had been made in southern Germany during the eleventh and twelfth centuries came into the possession of the Augsburg collector Konrad Peutinger, whose name it now bears. Even then the complicated history of the map was not complete: after Peutinger's death in 1547 the map was again lost until 1591 when part of it was found by Marcus Welser, who had it engraved and published. Seven years later, however, the entire map was recovered and taken to the great cartographer Abraham Ortelius, who was responsible for its publication. The *Peutinger Table* is a highly interesting document, though diagrammatic in conception. It appears on a roll 21 feet by

1 foot (6.4 metres by 0.3 metre) in dimensions, a format which could not fail to result in gross distortions of shape and spatial relationships. However, it was highly practicable in the field, being light and portable. The main aim of its maker was to focus the map firmly on the communications network of the Roman Empire and the distances between cities and garrisons. Roads appear as thin red lines and settlements are shown pictorially in perspective.

Apart from the *Peutinger Table* the main evidence of Roman mapmaking consists of some sketch maps in *Notitia Dignitatum Imperii Romani* (fifth century AD).

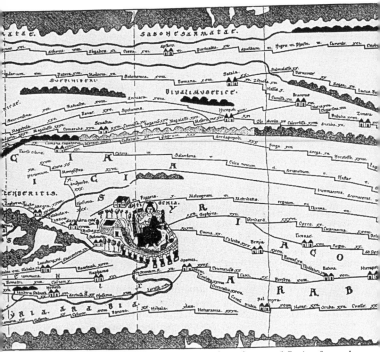

*A section, showing the city of Antioch and part of Syria, from the 'Tabula Peutingeriana' or 'Peutinger Table', a road map of the Roman Empire which came into the possession of Konrad Peutinger of Augsburg, after whom it takes its name. This section is reproduced from an illustration in Konrad Miller's 'Itineraria Romana' (Stuttgart, 1916). Courtesy: University of Liverpool.*

## Medieval route maps

During the medieval period route maps were required, not so much for military or administrative purposes, but to meet the needs of pilgrims travelling to the great religious centres of Europe and the Holy Land. Accounts of these ambitious journeys are contained in itineraries such as *Peregrinatio in Terram Sanctam* by Bernhard von Breydenbach (Mainz, 1486), which relates the author's experiences on a journey to the Holy Land in 1483. A map of Palestine appeared in this work together with various views of cities and observations on the manners and customs of Palestine.

Two centuries earlier Matthew Paris, the monastic historian of St Albans, prepared an itinerary, his *Chronica Majora* (1259), which contained a pictorial route map designed to show in vertical strip maps the pilgrimage route from London to the Holy Land. The strip-map method was later used to great effect by John Ogilby in the seventeenth century and is still in use. Matthew Paris's more familiar works are the four versions of a map of Britain which concentrate on the pilgrim route from Newcastle in the north to Dover. The best of the four provides a recognisable view of Britain though it was necessary to distort shape and relationships in order to display the pilgrim way vertically down the centre of the country. Although roads are not delineated on the maps the route can easily be followed from the many monastic sites which Matthew located along it. In contrast with normal medieval practice, Matthew's maps are oriented to the north.

## The Gough or Bodleian Map

This remarkable map, known either as the Gough Map after its discoverer, Richard Gough, or the Bodleian Map from its location in Oxford's Bodleian Library, was prepared by an anonymous mapmaker around 1360. It is a landmark in British cartographic development, not only for its immediately recognisable and accurate delineation of Britain's coasts, but for its depiction of the network of roads. Indeed it is believed that the general accuracy of the map owes much to its construction on a framework resulting from a precise plotting of the road system. In this it differs fundamentally from the Matthew Paris maps in which the delineation of the topography has been adjusted to the basic conception of placing the pilgrim route in a vertical straight line; in the case of the Gough Map the roads provide the basis of an accurate depiction of the topography. Perhaps the most curious feature of the map is the north-south elongation of Scotland and a corresponding east-west contraction. The roads are drawn as straight lines joining the town symbols; towns and other settlements are shown pictorially, the least important by a single simple building, those at the top of the scale – over forty walled towns – by a group of buildings, churches with a spire or tower, crenellated walls and houses. Rivers, which were an aid to communication, are numerous and in the fashion of the time over-prominent; in contrast, hills which hindered travel, are paid little attention; forests are shown by a symbol comprising two intertwining trees. It is assumed that the map was designed for practical use by travellers, possibly by government couriers and other officials of the Crown.

## The European scene

In France several roadbooks and itineraries have survived. A complex network of French post roads, coupled with a constant supply of post horses and guides for travellers, date back to an *Ordonnance* made by Louis XI in 1464. It is to Nuremburg in Germany, however, that we have to turn for the earliest printed road map. This was a woodcut made by an instrument maker, Erhard Etzlaub, which was designed to assist pilgrims travelling to Rome for the Holy Year celebrations in 1500. Known as the *Rom Weg* or *Rome Way*, it bore the lengthy title '*Das ist der Rom Weg von Meylen zu meylen mit punkten verzeichnet von eyner stat zu der endern durch deutsche lantt*' ('The way to Rome, marked out with dots from one town to the next through German lands'). Oddly oriented to the south so that Rome appears at the top, the map featured small circles to locate towns with dotted lines indicating the most propitious routes between them. The distance between dots was one German mile or about 7 km.

In Britain roadbooks of a kind existed though they were confined to verbal descriptions of the routes and did not include maps. Among such works were the *Itinerary* of John Leland (*c.*1535-45), Raphael Holinshed's *Chronicles of England, Scotland and Ireland* (1577) and William Smith's *Particular Description of England* (1588).

Johannes Metellus Sequanus, who lived in Louvain and for a lengthy period in Cologne, prepared a traveller's atlas in four parts entitled *Itinerarium Orbis Christian* (1579-80). This is regarded as the first printed road atlas and is noteworthy in pioneering the use of double parallel lines to delineate roads. Mapmakers had generally accepted that some type of linear symbolisation was necessary to indicate roads but one interesting deviation from this practice is seen in *Codex Tepetlaoztoc*, a mid sixteenth-century work in which Mexican mapmakers drew rows of footprints to represent tracks – an evocative, though imprecise, technique.

## John Ogilby's Britannia

In 1675 there was a major advance in road mapping for in that year John Ogilby published *Britannia*, a monumental work containing one hundred plates on which the principal roads of England and Wales were displayed in strip-map form, a technique pioneered by Matthew Paris centuries earlier. Ogilby's work, which set a pattern for route mapping which has continued to this day, was sophisticated in conception and design. It was based on a sound systematic survey of the roads of Britain; it did away with

*A section of John Ogilby's strip map of the road from Bristol to Weymouth from 'Britannia' (1675). Courtesy: University of Liverpool.*

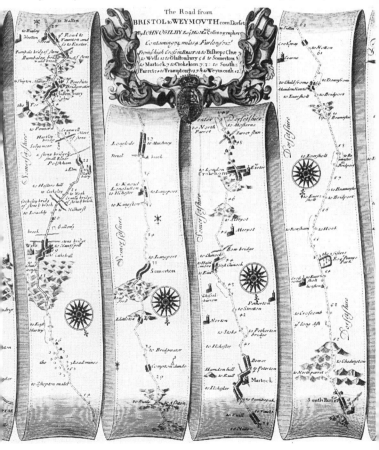

the use of local 'customary' miles and used the statute mile of 1760 yards which had been introduced by statute as far back as 1593; it established the one inch to one mile scale as a standard, which was not replaced by metric scales until the late 1960s and 1970s. The impact of *Britannia* on ensuing roadbooks was such that only derivatives appeared until John Cary made a new survey at the close of the eighteenth century. The great merit of Ogilby's strip-map technique as a means of conveying route information to a road traveller was that his attention was concentrated on the route itself – little extraneous detail was provided away from the road to distract him. *Britannia* also had its effect on county mapmaking for, after Ogilby's time, it became customary to include roads. Robert Morden in 1676 published sets of playing cards, each card bearing a tiny county map in which the roads were based on Ogilby. These, however, were more of a curiosity than serious maps and credit for the first set of county maps to bear roads is normally given to Morden's fine set prepared for Edmund Gibson's translation of Camden's *Britannia* (1695).

## Successors to Britannia

Despite the bulk of Ogilby's *Britannia*, which made it more suitable for planning a journey beforehand than for use *en route*, forty-four years were to pass before the appearance of a more portable, compact volume. As more and more people began to travel, demand rose for easily transportable atlases and roadbooks which could conveniently be taken on a journey. In 1719 and 1720 three such volumes were published. In the preface to the first of these – *A Pocket Guide to the English Traveller* (1719) by Thomas Gardner – Gardner says of Ogilby: 'As the original Plates are in large Sheets, the general Use of them has been hitherto lost, and the Book rather an Entertainment for the Traveller within Doors, than a Guide to him upon the Road'. In the same year John Senex published a quarto atlas entitled *An Actual Survey of all the Principal Roads of England and Wales; Described by One Hundred Maps from Copper Plates...First perform'd and publish'd by John Ogilby, Esq.; And now improved, very much corrected, and made portable by John Senex.* The third and best-known of these three roadbooks based on Ogilby is *Britannia Depicta or Ogilby Improv'd* (1720), a quarto volume with 273 plates bearing strip maps by the distinguished engraver Emanuel Bowen and text by John Owen. This work included small county maps in addition to the strip road maps. The latter are clear, attractive and very popular with present-day collectors.

Some roadbooks and itineraries concerned with Scottish and Irish roads appeared in the latter half of the eighteenth century.

The ROAD from
NOTTINGHAM TO GRIMSBY IN
LINCOLN SHIRE. *Containing 50 Comp & 67½ Meas⁴ M.*

From Nottingham

| | Comp Meas | | Comp Meas |
|---|---|---|---|
| to Newark | 12 17½ | to Stanton | 40 54½ |
| LINCOLN | 24 32½ | Briggesly | 40 61 6 |
| Walton | 26 38½ | Grimsby | 50 67½ |
| Market Raising | 36 48½ | | |

*'The road from Nottingham to Grimsby', a small map from John Owen and Emanuel Bowen's roadbook, 'Britannia Depicta' (1720).*

89

*Section of the road from York to Chester from Owen and Bowen's 'Britannia Depicta' (1720). The strip maps in this atlas are reduced from those in Ogilby's 'Britannia' with the aim of making a handier, more portable atlas.*

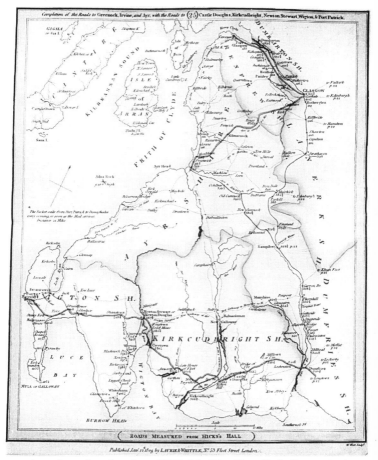

*A road map from Laurie and Whittle's 'New Traveller's Companion' (third edition, corrected to 1809).*

In 1776 George Taylor and Andrew Skinner published *Survey and Maps of the Roads of North Britain, or Scotland* and, in 1778, *Taylor and Skinner's Maps of the Roads of Ireland, surveyed 1777.* The latter is an octavo volume with 288 pages of road maps and tables of distances. The Scottish volume contains sixty-one plates by a variety of engravers, each plate bearing three narrow strips of roads, clearly and attractively depicted.

## *John Cary and other makers of roadbooks*

It was the engraver, mapseller and globe maker John Cary (1754-1835) who made the most significant contribution, not only to the mapping of British roads but also to the art of mapmaking in eighteenth- and early nineteenth-century Britain. Cary received a commission from the Postmaster-General to make an accurate survey of the road network of England, a task which involved some 10,000 miles (16,000 km) of measurement. For this task Cary was paid the rather niggardly sum of ninepence per mile but enjoyed exclusive rights to publish the results of his survey. This came to fruition in the first edition of his *New Itinerary* (1798), a highly successful roadbook which achieved eleven editions between 1798 and 1828.

Cary experienced strong competition from Daniel Paterson, assistant to the Quartermaster-General of His Majesty's Forces, who published *A New and Accurate Description of all the Direct and Principal Cross Roads in Great Britain* (1771). There were eighteen editions of this roadbook between 1771 and 1826, from which date until 1832 it was 'remodelled, augmented and improved' by Edward Mogg. The Mogg editions include a large amount of descriptive detail about the places and countryside *en route*. Another rival of Cary was Charles Smith, who produced *A New Pocket Companion* in 1826. *Laurie and Whittle's New Traveller's Companion* first appeared in 1806, with subsequent editions in 1810, 1814, 1828 and 1834. This volume contains twenty-four hand-coloured road maps, clearly engraved with distances from London indicated along each Direct Road. On the Cross Roads distances from one market town to another are indicated. Other useful information provided by Laurie and Whittle includes canals, rivers, ferry boats, packet boats etc. The author's advertisement states that 'The principal credit that the author attaches to himself...arises from the ease with which the traveller may hereby find his way from the metropolis to any part of the kingdom, as far north as Edinburgh and Glasgow, thence to Aberdeen, and from one market town to another'. Interestingly, the orientation varies from map to map in order to show the area under consideration to best advantage on the page.

# 9
# *Marine charts*

In classical times the most important aid available to navigators in the Mediterranean basin was the *periplus* or coastal pilot, a book of sailing directions based on accounts of particular voyages and containing information about the nature of coastlines, about harbours and the distance from one harbour to another. Later *peripli* included more specific information concerning tides, wind directions and hazards such as dangerous rocks and sandbanks. The invention of the magnetic compass in Italy in the early thirteenth century revolutionised navigation and *peripli* acquired a new sophistication. They were transformed into navigational guides called *portolani* which provided written information about coastlines, harbours and hazards together with, in some later examples, profile drawings of coastlines and plans of harbours. Maintained by mariners, *portolani* were a valuable storehouse of the practical knowledge and experience of their makers.

By 1300 *portolani* were supplemented by charts which transformed the written sailing directions into a graphic display, usually prepared on vellum with the neck on the left and having as their most striking feature a network of *rhumb lines* or lines of constant bearing which radiated over the entire area from a system of compass roses. The purpose of the rhumb lines was to enable the mariner to set a course from harbour to harbour using dividers and straight edge. Production of portolan charts was centred on Genoa and Venice and the Spanish ports of Barcelona and Palma. Italian charts usually covered an area including the Mediterranean and Black Seas while Spanish work extended further north into Scandinavia and northern Europe.

Conventionally the portolan charts located a great number of coastal places, their names drawn inland from the coast and at right angles to it. Ports were named in red, other places in black. The earliest extant portolan chart is the *Carte Pisane* or Pisan Chart (1300) and the earliest to include a date is by Petrus Visconte (1311). The zenith of Catalan cartography was attained in 1375 in the form of the *Catalan Atlas* prepared by two Majorcan Jews, Abraham Cresques and his son, Jafudo. Commissioned by Don Juan, son of the king of Aragon, the Cresques produced a work of cartographic artistry which extended the range of the conventional portolan to take in the whole of Asia. In so doing they used the techniques of portolan chartmaking for Europe and the Mediterranean and combined this with the Ptolemaic tradition for Asia. In 1381 the *Catalan Atlas* was presented to Charles VI of France.

*A detail from a beautiful late Portolan chart of 1569 which has been attributed to the Homem family of Portugal. Courtesy: University of Liverpool (MS.F.4.3).*

During the early decades of the sixteenth century the nautical chart developed in various directions, particularly in the inclusion of graduated scales of latitude and longitude, but, as yet, meridians and parallels were not carried across the face of the chart. Later charts extended the area well beyond the Mediterranean and Black Seas, using information gleaned from new discoveries around the African coasts and India, and eventually the eastern seaboard of North America was encompassed. In Portugal sumptuous charts were produced, largely as a consequence of the presence of the renowned school of navigation set up at Sagres by Prince Henrique, more familiarly known as Henry the Navigator. Beautiful charts, often virtual world maps, were prepared by Pedro and Jorge Reinel, Diogo and Lopo Homem and, especially, by Diego Ribeiro, whose splendid world chart (1529) marked the very peak of portolan tradition.

Elsewhere, Catalan chartmakers, notably the Oliva family, produced decorative charts which often departed from the earlier tradition of drawing on a single piece of vellum and were drawn on smaller sheets and then bound into book form. In Genoa Battista Agnese prepared over sixty atlases of this kind. Eventually charts became so richly decorative that they were clearly not designed for practical navigation at sea. The first *printed* chart intended solely for use at sea was a woodcut by the Venetian G. A. Vavassore, and the earliest strictly practical chart to be engraved on copper was prepared by Diogo Homem and printed in Venice in 1569. Hence-forward copper engraving became the standard method of producing sea charts as well as land maps. It remained so for three and a half centuries.

## Isolario

A rather different type of navigational aid appeared in Italy during the fifteenth and sixteenth centuries. This was the *Isolario* or book of islands, which allied text to graphic display using rather stylised maps of islands and plans of harbours and ports. Cristoforo Buondelmonte's *Liber Insularem Archipelagi* (Florence, 1420) is the earliest surviving example and, though never printed, it served as the prototype for later examples. The first printed island book was that of Bartolomeo dalli Sonetti, whose *Isolario* (*c*.1485) contained forty-nine charts, many of which included a scale of distance and used a symbol of a cross or a cross with four dots to locate offshore rocks.

## Northern Europe

Mercator's eighteen-sheet world chart (1569), constructed on his famous projection, was a major advance in aids to navigation but it was not until 1646 that the first actual collection of charts based on the Mercator projection was published. This was the sea

LIBRO                    SECONDO      XXX

*A bird's eye view of Venice and its lagoon from Benedetto Bordone's 'Isolario' (Venice, 1547 edition). Island books such as this were designed to aid mariners and the view of Venice emphasises the canal system as well as showing outstanding landmarks. Courtesy: University of Liverpool (Ryl.N.2.30).*

atlas by Sir Robert Dudley entitled *Dell' Arcano del Mare*, which contained 130 sea charts together with sailing directions, information about marine instruments and instructions for finding longitude.

The first printed sea atlas was the two-part *De Spieghel der Zeevaert* or *Mariner's Mirror* (1584) by the Dutch hydrographer Lucas Janszoon Waghenaer. This handsome atlas contained forty-four charts beautifully engraved and ornamented by the brothers Baptist and Johannes van Deutecum. It was printed in Antwerp at the renowned printing house of Christopher Plantin. The charts included soundings, the location of anchorages, dangerous rocks and buoys. Profiles of the coast were provided to show it as it would appear when seen by a mariner from a vessel sailing parallel to it. A certain amount of topographical detail – towns, hills, fields, woodland – was noted. Lavish ornamentation in the shape of elaborate cartouches, sea monsters and sailing vessels may have been a distraction from the charts' main purpose as navigational aids but added to their aesthetic appeal. The importance of Waghenaer's work was quickly recognised in Britain, where Anthony Ashley brought out a translation of the 1586 Latin edition under the title of *The Mariner's Mirror* (1588). This became so successful that henceforward all similar collections of charts became known as 'waggoners'. Surprisingly Waghenaer seemed content to rest on his laurels and made little effort to update his work or reprint it. He faced fierce competition from Dutch publishers and Willem Janszoon Blaeu issued a much superior sea atlas, *Het Licht der Zeevaert* (1608), which ran into at least twenty editions. Blaeu made some improvements of his own, adding more beacons, buoys and lights and transferring the coastal profiles from the face of the charts to the accompanying text.

Other Dutch publishers entered the field: Jan Jansson published sea atlases from 1620; Jacob Artz Colom and his son Arnold, Pieter Goos and Hendrik Doncker were all active in the late seventeenth century. Doncker began a new trend by including charts of waters outside Europe in his *Zeeatlas* but it was Johannes van Keulen who published the finest work of the period with his five-volume *Zee-Fakkel* or *Sea Torch* in 1684. This atlas contained charts and text which surpassed the work of any of van Keulen's contemporaries. Editions were published in Dutch, French and Spanish and a sixth volume appeared in 1753 with charts relating to navigation in East Asian waters.

Amsterdam's supremacy in chartmaking was unchallenged. English mariners depended on English editions of Dutch sea atlases and in France the same was true of French editions. Nevertheless some excellent English atlases did appear, John Sellers's *The English Pilot* (1671-2), for instance, and notably the *Great Britain's Coasting Pilot* (1693) by Captain Greenvile Collins. The latter contained forty-eight admirably clear and attractive plates which were based on a survey of Britain's coasts and harbours commissioned by the Admiralty. Despite some adverse criticism relating to inaccuracies, at least twelve further editions appeared between 1693 and 1792.

With the French taking a new scientific approach to cartography in the late seventeenth century, culminating in the great triangulation and survey of France by Cassini de Thury, it was hardly surprising that an atlas of sea charts which were superior to those of Collins was prepared and published by Charles Pene under the authorisation of Louis XIV and entitled *Le Neptune François* (1693). Not to be outdone, the Dutch, in the person of the Amsterdam publisher Pierre Mortier, collaborated with Hubert Jaillot of Paris in a counterfeit edition which was published in French, Dutch and English. The major significance of *Le Neptune François* lay in the new precision with which coastlines were delineated, the result of

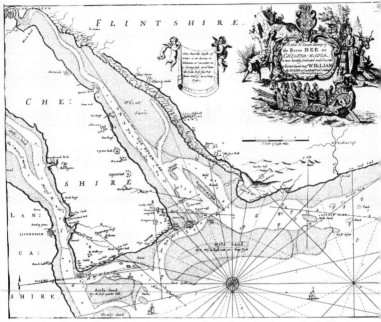

*A handsome chart of the Dee estuary from Captain Greenvile Collins's 'Great Britain's Coasting Pilot' (1693). Courtesy: University of Liverpool.*

tying in coastal features to the Cassini land survey. Numerous sea atlases were published in eighteenth-century France, notably by J. M. Bellin, whose finest work is *Le Petit Atlas Maritime* (1764).

The problem of determining longitude at sea was unsolved until John Harrison developed his successful marine chronometer in 1763, thus paving the way for the making of more accurate, larger-scale charts. This was one of several areas of British achievement during the eighteenth century. A splendid survey of the coasts from Anglesey to Cumberland was made by Samuel Fearon and John Eyes in 1736-7; the dedication on this chart to the 'Mayor and…Merchants of Liverpool' is an indication of the support of local shipping and business interests. Lewis Morris, a Holyhead customs officer, proposed a survey in direct competition to that of Fearon and Eyes but was eventually confined to coverage of the coast between Llandudno and Milford Haven in *Plans of Harbours, Bars, and Roads in St George's Channel* (1748).

The publication of charts in eighteenth-century Britain was generally left to private firms, including Mount and Page, Sayer and Bennett, Laurie and Whittle, Emanuel Bowen and William Faden. The Scottish surveyor Murdoch McKenzie, however, benefited from Admiralty backing in his accurate, detailed survey of the Orkneys (1750) and, later, in his more far-reaching survey *A Maritim Survey of Ireland and West Coast of Britain* (1766). McKenzie's *modus operandi* was to extend an accurate land survey, in which a network of triangles was constructed on a measured baseline, out to sounding locations established within sight of his shore positions, which were marked by beacons. His survey methods, as laid down in his *Treatise on Maritim Surveying* (1770), were an important step forward in British hydrography. Indeed Britain played a leading role in late eighteenth-century marine surveying. *Atlantic Neptune* by J. F. W. Des Barres, a British subject and military engineer of Swiss extraction, was a superb collection of charts published in 1784 in four sections: Nova Scotia, New England, Gulf and River of St Lawrence, and New York to the Gulf of Mexico. Designed 'for the use of the Royal Navy of Great Britain', the charts include a wealth of topographical detail as well as marine information. The entire collection was compiled from the work of numerous surveyors but Des Barres gave little credit to those surveyors whose work he published along with his own charts.

By the early nineteenth century the image of the world was being changed by adventurers such as Cook, who, with his Pacific voyages, disproved the theory of a great southern continent, the Terra Australis. Matthew Flinders charted most of the coastline of Australia and George Vancouver showed through his American surveys that there was no easily navigable North-West Passage to be opened up from the Pacific coast.

In 1795 the British Hydrographic Office was established with Alexander Dalrymple as its head. The first Admiralty chart was issued in 1801. British survey ships became an established part of the fleet and in 1808 Thomas Hurd, who replaced Dalrymple as Hydrographer of the Navy, ensured a regular supply of up-to-date charts to naval stations everywhere. In 1829 Admiral Sir Francis Beaufort took over and gradually established a chartmaking office which was a model for all others. During the nineteenth century the official Admiralty charts gradually superseded those of the private hydrographers in Britain. In the USA a strange situation arose in which two separate agencies, the US Hydrographic Office and the US Coast and Geodetic Survey, were engaged in chartmaking. Their operations involved some important innovations, particularly in the field of colour printing and, in general, their work was in advance of contemporary European production.

# 10
# *Cartographical oddities*

We are so familiar today with maps of considerable scientific accuracy presented graphically in atlases or on sheets of paper that it is possibly a little surprising to note the numerous different materials on which maps have been prepared throughout cartographic history – even after the availability of paper for the purpose. The clay tablet maps of the Babylonians, small enough to be held in the palm of the hand, have already been mentioned; so too has the bronze age Bedolina map carved into the face of a rock in northern Italy; North American Indians drew maps on birch bark or deer skins; Greenland Eskimos carved maps in wood and in so doing attempted to illustrate relief features; in early Mexican cartography maps were prepared on a material woven from agave fibre; the peoples of the Marshall Islands in the Pacific Ocean made charts which were built up from the ribs of palm leaves, tied together with threads of coconut fibre, which indicated the direction of the wave fronts.

Turning to more recent times, maps have frequently formed part of the design of commemorative plates and mugs; they have been produced on articles made in silver and glass and in the heyday of the railway system maps were often produced on tiles to show the rail network of particular companies. Examples may still be seen in a few stations, York and Whitby for instance.

While mapmakers in general have had serious practical aims in making their maps – the accurate portrayal of the earth's surface or a portion of it; to show the location of places; to indicate routes from one place to another; to illustrate the physical nature of a region, or its geology, its vegetation, its climate and so on – they have not always been quite so academic in their intentions. At various times mapmakers have been seen in the role of maker of educational games such as dissected puzzles, as political satirist, as caricaturist producing maps in the shape of animals or strange human beings, as maker of playing cards and as maker of maps of fictional or fantasy lands.

### *Dissected maps*
Modern pictorial jigsaw puzzles, with their beautifully photographed, 'chocolate box' type themes and their hundreds, even thousands, of pieces, originated around 1760 as very simple dissected maps. The dissected puzzle was invented by a Covent Garden map dealer, John Spilsbury, who mounted existing

100

engraved, hand-coloured maps on to mahogany sheets and with a fine-toothed saw cut along national and county boundaries. His idea in producing dissected maps was to further geographical education in an entertaining way – his trade card referred to 'All sorts of dissected maps for teaching geography'. Spilsbury listed two prices, both quite expensive for the time, of 10s 6d for a superior puzzle or 7s 6d 'without the sea', the sea being regarded as of only minor importance. Following Spilsbury's early death in 1769 at the age of twenty-nine other mapmakers turned to the lucrative production of dissected maps. The well-known mapmaker John Wallis claimed to be the 'original Manufacturer of Dissected Maps and Puzzles', either ignoring Spilsbury's prior claims or being unaware of his existence. He stated also that his '...dissected articles are superior both in correctness and workmanship to any in London. Wallis's major rival for an extensive period was another well-known mapmaker, William Darton, while the catalogue of Bowles and Carver (1795) includes ten dissected maps designed '...for teaching young Ladies and Gentlemen the Geography of the World, or any particular part thereof, in an easy and entertaining manner'.

## The use of maps in educational games

Maps have been used for more than three centuries in early board games. Gillian Hill[9] describes a game entitled *Le Jeu du Monde* (1645) in which sixty-three circles, each containing a tiny map of a country, are arranged in a spiral shape. Two dice were used, the objective being to reach the final circle, which contained a map of France. In England board games of this type involving maps were common in the later decades of the eighteenth century. John Jefferys published *A Journey through Europe*, which served as a prototype for many ensuing dice games involving maps. Originally such games had little to do with education but there came a gradual realisation that learning need not be at all tedious but could be amusing and entertaining. As a consequence map games were more and more frequently introduced into the family circle and the classroom. In Britain it was natural that the areas most commonly portrayed in board games were the world, Europe and Great Britain. Respectable cartographic publishers were often involved: the excellent Thomas Jefferys, for instance, maker of many fine large-scale county maps in the eighteenth century, published a game entitled *The Royal Geographical Pastime* (1770) as well as the first known dated game, *A Journey through Europe* (1759), and others. John Wallis, publisher of numerous maps and atlases, issued games such as the *Picturesque Round Game of the Produce and*

*Manufactures of the Counties of England and Wales, Wallis's Tour of England and Wales* and *Wallis's New Game: Wanderers in the Wilderness.* Later his son Edward published *Wallis's New Railway Game.* The early games had been engraved on copper and coloured laboriously by hand but the introduction of chromolithography meant that colour printing was readily available and the map games became more attractive and more sophisticated in presentation, often featuring delightful pictorial illustrations of the places encountered as the players made their way round the course to the finishing point.

### Playing-card maps

Nowadays it would be distinctly unusual to associate packs of playing cards with geographical education but in 1590 one W.B. (Skelton[10] describes his identity as unknown but suggests he may have been William Barlow while Gillian Hill describes W.B. as being William Bowes), realising that the total number of counties in England and Wales, fifty-two, was the same as the number of cards, produced sixty cards engraved on four plates; thirteen of the cards on each plate corresponded to the cards in one suit, the extra two consisting of an introductory card and a card bearing doggerel verse. Each of the fifty-two main cards carried a thumb-nail map of a particular county in a central rectangular panel. These maps are naturally sparse in detail, showing only the county boundary by a dotted line, the principal towns, main rivers and a few hills and some woodland. At the top and bottom of each card are four lines of descriptive text about the county, listing such information as area, length and breadth, and the major commodities. Bowes published a further set of playing cards bearing maps in *c.*1605.

In 1676 the well-known mapmaker Robert Morden published a set of playing cards bearing maps (these have been excellently reproduced in facsimile by Harry Margary, Lympne Castle, Kent, in 1972). The set consists of two introductory cards, the first bearing a general map of England and Wales with the counties delineated by dotted lines and initial letters or abbreviations: Y for Yorkshire; Norf for Norfolk, and so on. The second card, headed 'The Explanation of these Cards', explains that 'The four Suites are the 4 parts of England, the 13 Northern Counties are Clubs, the Western are Spades, the Eastern are Hearts, and the Southern are Diamonds'. Each of the main cards is subdivided into three panels, the top one including the value in figures on the left, sometimes hidden by the suit mark, which is crudely hand-stencilled; the name of the county; and, on the right, the value of the card in Roman numerals or for kings the head of Charles II, for queens that of Catherine of Braganza, and for knaves a variety of unspecified male heads. The map itself appears in the large central panel and shows scale, north point, county boundary, main towns shown either by an open circle or a building drawn in elevation and lettered in full, roads (after John Ogilby's *Britannia* of 1675), either by single or double lines, some hills, rivers and the names of adjoining counties. Unlike the maps on the W.B. series of playing cards, which are drawn to a uniform scale throughout, Morden's scales vary from map to map. In the bottom panel of each card Morden provides figures showing the length, breadth and circumference of the county, the latitude of the principal town and its distance from London, first in 'Reputed miles' and secondly in 'Measured Miles by Esqr Ogilby'. There are considerable discrepancies in the two figures. For instance the reputed miles from Cardigan to London are given as 147 miles but the measured miles are 219. In many counties Morden's playing card maps have the distinction of being the first county maps to show roads. Two more issues of the cards appeared in 1676 and in 1680 there was a further edition in which the cards were sold in the form of a small atlas entitled *A Pocket Book of all the Counties of England and Wales.* No further editions appeared in the seventeenth century but in 1773 H. Turpin published *A Brief Description of England and Wales* with the cards appearing opposite descriptive text and no longer of any use as playing cards.

In 1676 William Redmayne published a pack of playing cards bearing maps under the title *Recreative Pastime by Card-play; Geographical, Chronological and Historiographical, of England and Wales.* As examples of cartography these little maps have nothing to commend them. Much of each map is obliterated by the large suit mark being clumsily placed in the centre of the map. In general the maps are distorted and show little more than the county boundary, county town, a few rivers and some randomly distributed woodland. There is some descriptive text on each card, badly arranged and in execrable calligraphy. These were the last playing cards to show county maps of England and Wales, apart from a series of cards issued by John Lenthall in 1717 which closely follow Morden's set, but European publishers issued various packs of cards often bearing maps of the countries of the world. French publishers such as Gilles de la Boissiere, P. Duval and N. de Fer all issued sets of this kind.

## Maps in the form of animals or humans

Many early cartographers delighted in the portrayal of exotic flora and fauna on the face of their maps but much of the depiction of strange animals, birds, sea monsters and so on has been derided as figments of the mapmaker's imagination. Dr Wilma George, however, has made a strong case[11] to show that cartographers were well aware of the world distribution of animals and that much of what they illustrated was correct. Some cartographers, however, did put their imagination to full use in depicting separate countries or even whole continents in the form of a person or animal.

Europe was depicted in the shape of a woman, firstly by Joannes Bucius in 1537, later by the geographer Sebastian Münster in editions of his famous *Cosmographia* between 1544 and 1628, and by Heinrich Bünting in *Itinerarium Sacrae Scripturae* or *Travels according to the Scriptures* in 1581. Bünting also produced two very strange woodcut maps: the first showed the world as a clover leaf with Jerusalem in a circle at the centre and Europe, Asia and Africa in separate sections; the second showed the continent of Asia in the form of the winged

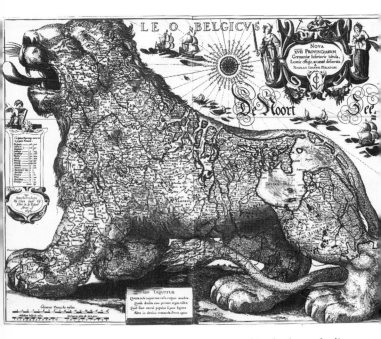

*'Leo Belgicus' – the Low Countries portrayed in the form of a lion. Numerous variations on this theme appeared, this fine example being by Nicholas Visscher and dating from 1650. By permission of the British Library (BL Maps C.9.d.1.(7)).*

horse, Pegasus. While the shape of the horse is quite realistically portrayed, the various land masses are grossly distorted and the overall configuration of the continent is initially difficult to comprehend. Much easier to appreciate are the famed series of animal maps known as *Leo Belgicus*. These interesting maps are based on a concept which originated with a plate in a history of the Low Countries, *De Leone Belgico* (1583), by an Austrian nobleman, Baron Michael von Eytzinger. The plate shows the seventeen provinces of the Netherlands enclosed within the realistically drawn shape of a lion. Little distortion was necessary to achieve this neatly, unlike the earlier woodcut map of Asia by Bünting, for example. The lion is seen half standing, his spine following the coastline, his right front paw raised and his tongue protruding from a wide open mouth. Eytzinger's idea was immediately popular and was seized upon by well-known cartographers such as Claes Jansz Visscher, Pieter van den Keere and Joannes van Deutecum. Some of the new versions followed Eytzinger closely, others used adaptations: for example, Famiano Strada produced a version in Rome in 1632 in which the lion's paw rested on a shield; Cornelius Jansson oriented the map differently, with west at the top, and drew his lion passant; Visscher produced two particularly attractive designs, the first with the lion in the Eytzinger pose facing north-east, the second with west at the top and the lion facing south-west. Each of Visscher's versions is noteworthy for the quality of the calligraphy and the lavish, beautifully designed cartouches and ornamentation.

During the eighteenth century numerous maps were produced in which countries were represented in human form; some of these were humorous caricatures such as the droll *Geography Bewitched: England and Wales* and *Geography Bewitched: Scotland* by Bowles and Carver. In these rather grotesque portrayals England and Wales are seen as a bucolic, pipe-smoking, beer-drinking male figure riding on a monstrous fish whose large head has an open mouth representing the Thames estuary and whose tail is Cornwall and Devon. Scotland is presented as a hunchbacked male resting on a cushion.

In the second half of the nineteenth century mapmakers turned to politics for inspiration in a number of political cartoon maps. One of the earliest and best of these, *The Evil Genius of Europe* (1859), is a rather pleasing map of Italy and parts of southern Europe in which the figure of a man – Napoleon III, whose head is partly concealed by the Swiss Alps – is struggling to pull on his boot, represented by Italy. The title placed at the top of the map in a separate panel is followed by the words: 'On a careful examination of this Panorama the Genius will be discovered struggling hard to pull on his Boot. It will be noticed, he has just put his foot in it. Will he be able to wear it?'

Geography Bewitched!
or a droll Caricature MAP of ENGLAND and WALES

*'Geography Bewitched – England and Wales' (1795). By permission of the British Library (BL Maps 54a, 26/1).*

## Maps of fictional or invented lands

The earliest known example of a map designed to portray a fictitious territory described in a literary work is a woodcut map of Sir Thomas More's *Utopia*. Made by an unknown artist, the first edition of this map was published at Louvain in 1516. It was followed by a second and a third edition, the last map being the work of Ambrosius Holbein, a less well-known elder brother of the renowned painter Hans Holbein. Not surprisingly, Holbein's map, again a woodcut, published in Basle in 1518, is superior in execution and more pleasing aesthetically. It is, however, less faithful to the descriptive details of More's text than the 1516 map.

Numerous other maps have been made to illustrate journeys through fictional lands, among them those which graphically portray John Bunyan's *The Pilgrim's Progress* (1678) and Jonathan Swift's *Gulliver's Travels* (1726).

## Maps of love and marriage

Maps dealing with romance and love were unfailingly popular, particularly during the eighteenth century, when the German cartographer Matthias Seutter made outstanding examples of the genre. The most splendid example of Seutter's love maps rejoices in the lengthy title *Representation Symbolique et Ingenieuse projettée en Siege et en Bombardement comme il faut empecher prudemment les attaques de L'Amour* (c.1730). The map, beautifully designed and engraved, features a great fortress, centrally placed. Here man is besieged on all sides by the bewitching forces of love. At the foot of the map is a lengthy legend in French and German referring to features on the map, in which capital letters or numbers are used to illustrate the method of defending and conserving the heart against the attacks of love.

Seutter, in addition to his love maps, also published a number of strange maps, one of which, entitled *Schlaraffenlande* (Land of Milk and Honey), is outstanding. It depicts this strange Utopia in which roasted pigs walk the streets with knives stuck into them so that the idle townsfolk could eat as they passed by. Similarly, birds fly already cooked waiting to be eaten. The map itself, immensely detailed, shows nineteen imaginary countries, each concerned with a specific vice. To the south is the ultimate destination of the dwellers in this land of sloth and vice – Hell!

Other maps based on the theme of love include *Das Reich der Liebe* (1777), published in Leipzig by J. G. I. Breitkopf. This map illustrates a man's travels from the Land of Youth, through areas such as the Land of Unhappy Love, the Desert of Melancholy and the Land of Lust.

*A section of the Madaba mosaic map of Palestine (AD 560) showing the city of Jerusalem. The mosaic when whole measured 25 by 5 metres and was composed of some two million pieces. It can be seen in the Greek Orthodox Church of St George in the small town of Madaba in Jordan.*

The *Matrimonial Map* (*c*.1820) is a British example of the genre, a rather simple map in which man, sailing on the Great Ocean of Love, is faced with various pitfalls such as the Rocks of Jealousy, the Rocks of Ice, and the Sands of Inconstancy. Having avoided the hazards of the seas, he achieves his goal but even on dry land the course of true love is far from smooth for he has to negotiate the dangers of the River Amour with its banks swarming with slow-worms and scorpions.

## Maps made on unusual materials
### Mosaic maps

The small town of Madaba in the Hashemite Kingdom of Jordan is famed as a centre of the mosaic industry and particularly for its unique mosaic map of Palestine and lower Egypt which was discovered during the building of the Greek Orthodox Church of St George in 1898. Parts of the map, which occupies a considerable portion of the floor of the church, have been lost but, considering the mosaic dates from AD *c*.560, much of it remains in a surprisingly legible condition. Originally it is thought to have measured some 25 metres by 5 metres and some two million pieces were used in its construction. The map features some 150 place-names and its most striking feature is a bird's eye view of Jerusalem in which streets, surrounding walls, gates and main buildings are clearly identifiable.

*Tapestry maps*

Maps as a subject for tapestries are extremely rare, the finest examples coming from the looms of William Sheldon at Barcheston Manor in Warwickshire and Beoley in Worcestershire in the sixteenth century. Aware of the advantages of using the wool of Cotswold sheep in the making of tapestries, Sheldon sent Richard Hicks of Barcheston to study in Flanders, where he learned the art of tapestry weaving. On his return to Barcheston c.1659 Hicks brought with him some Flemish weavers and Barcheston Manor became England's first major tapestry-manufacturing establishment. Among the magnificent tapestries produced there were the renowned tapestry maps showing parts of English counties. Roughly based on Saxton in style and content, the maps include rivers with the important bridging points, woodland prominently depicted by groups of nicely woven trees, hills, and towns named and symbolised by groups of buildings shown in elevation. Examples of the Sheldon tapestry maps are on display at the Victoria and Albert Museum in London.

*Map samplers*

One does not readily associate maps with needlework but there was considerable interest in producing sampler maps in the late eighteenth century. Their popularity reflected a greater interest on the part of the general public in geography and travel. As communications improved there was a consequent widening of people's horizons, education became ever more important and the making of map samplers was seen as an effective way of imparting geographical knowledge to young people at the same time as they learned the art of needlework.

Thomas Jefferys, who issued a reprint of Christopher Saxton's county maps in 1749, and John Spilsbury, whose pioneering work with dissected maps has already been mentioned, were instrumental in providing a new stimulus for embroiderers. Spilsbury, ever inventive, conceived the idea of printing the outlines of maps on to white silk or satin. Some of these samplers were then worked in black thread, possibly in an attempt to resemble as closely as possible the detail of the original engraving; others were worked in various colours. While maps of England and Wales showing counties were the most popular, some children produced maps of the counties in which they lived and maps of European countries, Africa or North

America were not uncommon. While some samplers were crude in appearance compared with the original maps – not surprisingly as the standards of achievement among the young ladies would vary considerably – others achieved high standards of lettering and line.

This final chapter has demonstrated that there are some unusual sides to mapmaking. Indeed, cartography is an immensely wide and varied field of interest which involves an inexhaustible range of topics and disciplines. To the collector, whether he be searching avidly for rare atlases, individual engraved maps, charts, roadbooks or unusual uses of maps, there is an immense quarry of fascinating material awaiting his attention.

# Further reading

The following general books are recommended to the amateur enthusiast:

Bagrow, Leo. *History of Cartography*. Watts, 1964.

Baynton-Williams, R. *Investing in Maps*. Barrie & Rockliff, 1969.

Beresiner, Yasha. *British County Maps. Reference and Price Guide*. Antique Collectors' Club, 1983.

Hodgkiss, A.G. *Understanding Maps: A Systematic History of Their Use and Development*. Dawson, 1981.

Lister, Raymond. *How to Identify Old Maps and Globes*. Bell, 1965.

Lister, Raymond. *Antique Maps and Their Cartographers*. Bell, 1970.

Moreland, Carl, and Bannister, David. *Antique Maps: A Collector's Handbook*. Longman, 1983.

Potter, Jonathan. *Collecting Antique Maps: An Introduction to the History of Cartography*. Studio Editions, 1988.

Radford, P.J. *Antique Maps*. Garnstone Press, 1971.

Tooley, R.V. *Maps and Mapmakers*. Batsford, fourth edition 1970.

Tooley, R.V., and Bricker, C. *History of Cartography – 2500 Years of Maps and Mapmakers*. Thames & Hudson, 1969.

Serious students and collectors of early maps and atlases who wish to delve deeper into the subject should find the following selection of works helpful:

Chambers, Betty. *Printed Maps and Town Plans of Bedfordshire 1576-1900*. Bedfordshire Historical Record Society, Bedford, 1983.

Harley, J.B. *Maps for the Local Historian: A Guide to the British Sources*. National Council of Social Service for the Standing Conference for Local History, 1972.

Harley, J.B. *The Historian's Guide to Ordnance Survey Maps*. National Council of Social Service for the Standing Conference for Local History, 1964.

Harvey, P.D.A. *The History of Topographical Maps: Symbols, Pictures and Surveys*. Thames & Hudson, 1980.

Hodgkiss, A.G., and Tatham, A.F. *Keyguide to Information Sources in Cartography*. Mansell, 1986.

Hodson, Donald. *County Atlases of the British Isles Published after 1703. Volume I. Atlases Published 1703-43*. The Tewin Press, 1984.

Hodson, Donald. *County Atlases of the British Isles Published after 1703. Volume II. Atlases Published 1743-63*. The Tewin Press, 1989.

Howse, Derek, and Sanderson, Michael. *The Sea Chart*. David & Charles, 1973.

Koeman, Ir C. *Collections of Maps and Atlases in the Netherlands; Their History and Present State*. E. J. Brill, 1961.

Koeman, Ir C. *Joan Blaeu and His Grand Atlas*. Philip, 1970.

Koeman, Ir C. *The Sea on Paper – The Story of the Van Keulens and their 'Sea-Torch'*. Theatrum Orbis Terrarum, 1972.

Moir, D.G. *The Early Maps of Scotland*. The Royal Scottish Geographical Society, 1973.

Robinson, A.H.W. *Marine Cartography in Britain: A History of the Sea Chart to 1855*. Leicester University Press, 1962.

Scott, Valerie G., and Barty-King, Hugh. *County Maps and Histories: Sussex*. Quiller Press, 1985.

Scott, Valerie G., and McLaughlin, Eve. *County Maps and Histories: Berkshire*. Quiller Press, 1984.

Scott, Valerie G., and McLaughlin, Eve. *County Maps and Histories: Buckinghamshire*. Quiller Press, 1984.

Scott, Valerie G., and Rook, Tony. *County Maps and Histories: Hertfordshire*. Quiller Press, 1989.

Shirley, Rodney W. *Early Printed Maps of the British Isles, 1472-1650*. Holland Press, 1980.

Shirley, Rodney W. *The Mapping of the World – Early Printed World Maps, 1472-1700*. Holland Press, 1983.

Skelton, R.A. *County Atlases of the British Isles, 1579-1703*. Carta Press, 1970.

Skelton, R.A. *Explorers' Maps*. Spring Books, 1958.

Smith, David. *Antique Maps of the British Isles*. Batsford, 1982.

Stevens, Henry. *Ptolemy's Geography: A Brief Account of All the Printed Editions down to 1730*. Theatrum Orbis Terrarum, undated.

Stone, Jeffrey. *Illustrated Maps of Scotland from Blaeu's Atlas Novus of the 17th Century*. Studio Editions, 1991.

Wallis, Helen, and Robinson, Arthur. *Cartographical Innovations: a Handbook of Mapping Terms to 1900*. Map Collector Publications, 1987.

Wilford, John Noble. *The Mapmakers. The Story of the Great Pioneers in Cartography – from Antiquity to the Space Age*. Junction Books, 1981.

Woodward, David (editor). *Five Centuries of Map Printing*. University of Chicago Press, 1975.

## Periodical publications

*The Map Collector* is a finely illustrated quarterly journal with scholarly articles entirely devoted to the interests of collectors of early maps. It is obtainable from Map Collector Publications Ltd, 44 High Street, Tring, Hertfordshire HP23 5BH.

*Imago Mundi* is an annual hardback publication issued free to members of the International Society for the History of Cartography. It is published by Imago Mundi Ltd, c/o Lympne Castle, Kent.

## Society for Map Collectors

The International Map Collectors' Society is a British organisation which is entirely concerned with the world of antique maps. Regular meetings are held in different parts of the United Kingdom and the world. The Society's quarterly publication, the *IMCoS Journal*, contains articles on early maps as well as news of current events, reports on meetings and so on. Information about the Society can be obtained from the General Secretary, W. H. W. Pearce, 29 Mount Ephraim Road, Streatham, London SW16 1NQ; telephone and fax: 0181-769 5041.

# Where to obtain and consult early maps

Important collections are housed in the Map Library of the British Library, the Royal Geographical Society, the National Maritime Museum, the Bodleian Library, Cambridge University Library and the National Library of Scotland. With the exception of the Royal Geographical Society, it is necessary to obtain special prior permission to consult maps in these establishments. Many university libraries and Departments of Geography also house collections of early maps but again it is necessary to obtain permission to consult items in such collections from the appropriate Librarian or Map Curator.

Some of the greatest treasures of early cartography are on public display. Examples include the famous Hereford Map in Hereford Cathedral; the World Map of Juan de la Cosa in the Naval Museum, Madrid; the renowned Madaba mosaic map, dating from AD *c*.560, which is housed in the Greek Orthodox Church of St George in the small town of Madaba in Jordan; the fresco maps in the Palazzo Vecchio, Florence, made by Egnazio Danti, 1563-75; and the marvellous series of maps of parts of Italy, also by Danti, in the Galleria del Belvedere in the Vatican.

## Specialist dealers in early maps

*Antique Maps and Prints*, 30 St Mary's Street, Stamford, Lincoln-shire PE9 2DL. Telephone: 01780 52330.

*Baynton-Williams*, 37A High Street, Arundel, West Sussex BN18 9AG. Telephone: 01903 883588.

*Benet Gallery*, 19 King's Parade, Cambridge CB2 1SP. Telephone: 01223 353783. Maps relating to Cambridge only.

*Billson of St Andrews*, 15 Greyfriars Garden, St Andrews, Fife KY16 9HG. Telephone and fax: 01334 475063.

*Brobury House Gallery*, Brobury, Herefordshire HR3 6BS. Telephone: 01981 500229.

*Clive A. Burden Ltd*, 46 Talbot Road, Rickmansworth, Hertford-shire WD3 1HE. For British maps, telephone and fax: 01923 778097. For overseas maps: telephone 01923 772387; fax 01923 896520.

*Carson Clark Gallery* (Scotia Maps), 173 Canongate, The Royal Mile, Edinburgh EH8 8BN. Telephone: 0131-556 4710.

*Corner Shop*, 5 St John's Place, Hay-on-Wye, Herefordshire. Telephone: 01497 820045.

*Susanna Fisher*, Spencer, Upham, Southampton SO32 1JD. Telephone 01489 860291. Fax: 01489 860638.

*J. A. L. Franks Ltd*, 7 New Oxford Street, London WC1A 1BA. Telephone: 0171-405 0274. Fax: 0171-430 1259.

*Frontispiece*, 40 Porters Walk, Tobacco Dock, London E1 9SF. Telephone: 0171-702 1678. Also at: Cabot Place East, Concourse Level, Canary Wharf, London E14 4QS. Telephone: 0171-363 6336.

*Harrington Brothers*, The Chelsea Antique Market, 253 King's Road, Chelsea, London SW3 5EL. Telephone: 0171-352 1720. Fax: 0171-823 3449. Also at Old Church Galleries, 320 King's Road, Chelsea, London SW3 5EP. Telephone: 0171-351 4649.

*Julia Holmes*, South Gardens Cottage, South Harting, near Petersfield, Hampshire GU31 5QJ. Telephone: 01730 825040. (By appointment only.)

*Hughes and Smeeth Ltd*, 1 Gosport Street, Lymington, Hampshire SO41 9BG. Telephone: 01590 676324.

*J. Alan Hulme*, 52 Mount Way, Waverton, Chester CH3 7QF. Telephone: 01244 336472.

*Ingol Maps and Prints*, Cantsfield House, 206 Tag Lane, Ingol, Preston, Lancashire PR2 3TX. Telephone: 01772 724769. (Postal business only.)

*King's Court Galleries*, 54 West Street, Dorking, Surrey RH4 1BS. Telephone: 01306 881757. Fax: 01306 75305. Also at 951/953 Fulham Road, London SW6 5HY. Telephone: 0171-610 6939. Fax: 0171-731 4737.

*Michael Lewis Gallery*, 17 High Street, Bruton, Somerset BA10 0AB. Telephone: 01749 813557.

*Maggs Bros Ltd*, 50 Berkeley Square, London W1X 6EL. Telephone: 0171-493 7160. Fax: 0171-499 2007.

*The Map House*, 54 Beauchamp Place, Knightsbridge, London SW3 1NY. Telephone: 0171-589 4325 or 0171-584 8559. Fax: 0171- 589 1041.

*Richard Nicholson of Chester*. Shop: 25 Watergate Street, Chester CH1 2LB. Correspondence to: Stoneydale, Pepper Street, Christleton, Chester CH3 7AG. Telephone: 01244 326818 (shop) or 01244 336004.

*Avril Noble*, 2 Southampton Street, Covent Garden, London WC2E 7HA. Telephone: 0171-240 1970.

*O'Flynn Antiquarian Books*, 35 Micklegate, York. Telephone: 01904 641404.

*Oldfield Gallery*, 76 Elm Grove, Southsea, Hampshire PO5 1LN. Telephone and fax: 01705 838042.

*O'Shea Gallery*, 120A Mount Street, London W1Y 5HB. Telephone: 0171-629 1122. Fax: 0171-629 1116.

*Jonathan Potter*, 125 New Bond Street, London W1Y 9AF. Telephone: 0171-491 3520. Fax: 0171-491 9754.

*Sanders of Oxford Ltd*, 104 High Street, Oxford OX1 4BW. Telephone: 01865 242590. Fax: 01865 721784.

*Henry Sotheran Ltd*, 80 Pimlico Road, London SW1W 8PL. Telephone: 0171-730 8756. Fax: 0171-823 6090.

*Tooley Adams and Company Ltd*, 13 Cecil Court, Charing Cross Road, London WC2N 4EZ. Telephone: 0171-240 4406. Fax: 0171-240 8058.

*Robert Vaughan Antiquarian Booksellers*, 20 Chapel Street, Stratford-upon-Avon, Warwickshire CV37 6EP. Telephone: 01789 205312.

*Warwick Leadley Gallery*, 5 Nelson Road, Greenwich, London SE10 9JB. Telephone: 0181-858 0317. Fax: 0181-853 1773.

*The Witch Ball Antiquarian Print and Map Shop*, 48 Meeting House Lane, Brighton, East Sussex BN1 1HB. Telephone: 01273 326618.

## *Map fair*

*The Antiquarian Map and Print Fair* is held monthly at the Bonnington Hotel, 92 Southampton Row, London WC1 4BH. Telephone: 0171-242 2828.

# *Footnotes*

1. Sir George Fordham, *Studies in Carto-Bibliography British and French*, Dawson, 1969; page 101.

2. F. G. Emmison and R. A. Skelton, 'The description of Essex by John Norden', *The Geographic Journal,* CXIII, part I, March 1957.

3. *The Large Scale County Maps of the British Isles, 1596-1850,* Elizabeth M. Rodger, Bodleian Library, Oxford, second edition 1972.

4. Reproduced in facsimile by the Worcestershire Historical Society, 1962, with text by J. B. Harley.

5. Colonel Sir Charles Close, *The Early Years of the Survey,* David & Charles reprint, 1969; page 2.

6. Ida Darlington and James Howgego, *Printed Maps of London circa 1553-1850*, Philip, 1964.

7. *Map Making to 1900; An Historical Glossary,* International Cartographic Association, 1976; page 13.

8. Bagrow, Leo, *History of Cartography*, Watts, London, 1964; pages 37-8.

9. Gillian Hill, *Cartographical Curiosities*, The British Library, 1978.

10. R. A. Skelton, *County Atlases of the British Isles*, Carta Press, London, 1970.

11. Wilma George, *Animals and Maps*, Secker & Warburg, 1969.

# *Index*

Page numbers in italic refer to illustrations.

# INDEX